MISSISSIPPI GODDAMN

Jonathan Norton

BROADWAY PLAY PUBLISHING INC
New York
www.broadwayplaypublishing.com
info@broadwayplaypublishing.com

Cover art by Andrea Markowski

First edition: April 2018
I S B N: 978-0-88145-772-8

Book design: Marie Donovan
Page make-up: Adobe InDesign
Typeface: Palatino

dedicated in memory of Dr Dennis Simon

MISSISSIPPI GODDAMN was commissioned by the Diaspora Performing Arts Commissioning Program, a project of the South Dallas Cultural Center.

MISSISSIPPI GODDAMN received its World Premiere by South Dallas Cultural Center (Producer, Vicki Meek) on 19 February 2015. The cast and creative contributors were as follows:

CHUCK .... Tyrees Allen
CLAUDETTE/MYRLIE EVERS ...... Whitney LaTrice Coulter
GERTIE ....Stormi Demerson
ROBERT-EARL ....Calvin Gabriel
JIMMIE/MEDGAR EVERS..............................Jamal Sterling
ROBBIE .... Ashley Wilkerson

Director .... vickie washington
Set design ....Rodney Dobbs
Costume design .... Rhonda Gorman
Lighting design & fight choreography ....Charlton Gavitt
Sound design...Catherine Luster
Properties design.. Sheri Nance
Dramaturgy .... Janice Franklin
Assistant director & stage manager ....Richard Quadri*

MISSISSIPPI GODDAMN is a recipient of a 2015 Artistic Innovations Grant from the Mid-America Arts Alliance.

MISSISSIPPI GODDAMN received a subsequent developmental production at Pyramid Theatre Company (Tiffany Johnson, Artistic Director; Ken-Matt Martin, Executive Director) in Des Moines, Iowa; opening on 27 July 2017. The cast and creative contributors were as follows:

CHUCK .... Edward M Barker
CLAUDETTE/MYRLIE EVERS .... DeShana Langford
ROBBIE .... Victoria O'Bryant
GERTIE .... Farica L Robertson
ROBERT-EARL .... Aaron Smith
JIMMIE/MEDGAR EVERS .... Antonio Woodard

Director .... Ken-Matt Martin
Set design .... Tom Lewis
Costume design .... Susanna Douthit
Lighting design/technical direction .... John Pomeroy
Sound design .... Josh Jepson
Properties design .... Catherine Gray
Assistant director .... Napoleon M Douglas
Production stage manager .... Paige Beck
Assistant stage manager .... Lexi Morrow

A NOTE ABOUT CASTING

The playwright requires that producers and directors adhere to the double casting as described in the script. The only exception to this is in the case of college/university productions. In those cases, MEDGAR and MYRLIE can be played by different actors than JIMMIE and CLAUDETTE for the purposes of giving more actors opportunities. However, the playwright strongly believes university productions should keep the double casting of JIMMIE/MEDGAR and CLAUDETTE/MYRLIE as it provides a great training opportunity for young actors.

CHARACTERS & SETTING

All the characters are African American

ROBBIE MONROE, *16 years old.* ROBBIE *is short for Roberta. She has a childhood scar on her palm. The scar should be on the hand the actress writes with.*

CLAUDETTE HOLLINS, *23 years old.* ROBBIE'*s older sister. The actress that plays* CLAUDETTE *also plays* MYRLIE EVERS *in ACT TWO.*

JIMMIE HOLLINS, *27 years old.* CLAUDETTE'*s husband. The actor that plays* JIMMIE *also plays* MEDGAR EVERS *in ACT TWO.*

GERTIE MONROE, *45.* ROBBIE *and* CLAUDETTE'*s mother. A schoolteacher.*

ROBERT-EARL MONROE, *47.* ROBBIE *and* CLAUDETTE'*s father, and* GERTIE'*s husband. A high school football coach.*

CHARLES "CHUCK" PRUITT, *47. Lives down the street from* ROBBIE'*s family. Owns a café. Friends call him Chuck or Pruitt.*

Jackson, Mississippi. ROBBIE'*s childhood home, right down the street from* MEDGAR EVERS' *house. A late fifties ranch style house.*

Time: ACT ONE: June 10–12, 1963
ACT TWO: Spring 1959

Is this America, the land of the free and the home of the brave, where we have to sleep with our telephones off of the hooks because our lives be threatened daily, because we want to live as decent human beings, in America?
Fannie Lou Hamer

ACT ONE

Scene One

(Lights up in the living/dining room of the MONROE's *mid-fifties ranch style house. Early evening but not dark yet.)*

(From the kitchen, we hear a dish shatter on the floor.)

CLAUDETTE: I'M GOING HOME!

GERTIE: CLAUDETTE!

*(*CLAUDETTE *storms out of the kitchen into the living room—followed by her mother,* GERTIE.*)*

CLAUDETTE: It was an accident. Leave me alone.

*(*GERTIE *speeds up and gets ahead of* CLAUDETTE. *She blocks the door.)*

GERTIE: This isn't over between us. I know one way or the other, you will come around. You love your little sister too much—

CLAUDETTE: Fine. I'll go back the other way.

*(*CLAUDETTE *turns and heads back to the kitchen.* GERTIE *speeds past her daughter again and blocks her a second time.* CLAUDETTE *turns to run to the front door but* GERTIE *ain't having it.)*

GERTIE: You got one more time to make me chase after you. And girl it's gonna be your last time.

*(*CLAUDETTE *sits.)*

GERTIE: Cross your legs.

(CLAUDETTE *crosses her legs.*)

CLAUDETTE: It's not fair. She causes all this trouble and what punishment does she get? She gets to go to California for the summer and frolic on the beach—

GERTIE: They let Negroes frolic on the beach in California?

CLAUDETTE: That's not all they let Negroes do in California, mama. California is no place for a sixteen year old girl. Especially *that* sixteen year old girl. And I do not have time to babysit my hateful and hard-headed kid sister. For three-months? And if she won't listen to you and daddy what makes you think she will listen to me?

GERTIE: You're her big sister. She idolizes you.

CLAUDETTE: She called me a blind, deaf and dumb, cog in the wheel of the White man's o-pression of the Negro in America.

(*Beat.* GERTIE *thinks.*)

GERTIE: Baby. It's only for the summer. She's sixteen. You know how sixteen year olds can be.

CLAUDETTE: I wouldn't wish that hellion on my worst enemy. The answer is no.
(*Jumps up. Getting bold*)
And Jimmy and I are in agreement. And I have to abide by my husband's wishes. So I don't know what else to tell you.
(*She goes to the front door to leave.*)
Goodnight, mother.

GERTIE: Those white boys still outside? Prowling?

CLAUDETTE: I'll take my chances.

GERTIE: Wait till your father comes home so he can—

(CLAUDETTE *opens the door to leave. Outside, a car speeds down the street. The Dixie horn slicing the air, all the way down the street—then the car breaks. She leans out the door and looks outside.*)

CLAUDETTE: (*Looking out*) Oh my God. They outside Medgar Evers' house. They're banging on his front door. Something bad about to happen.

GERTIE: Get in this house.

(CLAUDETTE *lets out a scream. She slams the door and runs to the kitchen*)

GERTIE: What happened?

CLAUDETTE: (*Poking her head into the living room*) One of the white boys, he saw me. And his licked his tongue out at me like a snake. Real nasty.

(GERTIE *goes to the window.*)

CLAUDETTE: Don't go to the window.

GERTIE: Nobody answering.
Please nobody be home.
Oh God. I'm too afraid to look.

(GERTIE *moves away from the door. A stretch of silence, interrupted by the Dixie horn. Then silence, again.*)

CLAUDETTE: What if they come here next?

GERTIE: Why would they—

CLAUDETTE: The newspaper.

(*There is a loud knock at the door. The women don't move. Another knock. Then another.* GERTIE *gestures for* CLAUDETTE *to hide. Then* GERTIE *disappears to her bedroom. Another knock.* GERTIE *comes back out with a shotgun.*)

CHUCK: (*O S*) GERTIE! GERTIE! Open the door.

(GERTIE *goes to the door. She yells out.*)

GERTIE: Don't yell at me. That's not the secret knock.

CHUCK: I forgot what it is. Just open the goddamn door.

(GERTIE *opens the door.* CHUCK *comes in dragging* ROBBIE *by the arm.)*

ROBBIE: Let go of me. Let go of me.

CHUCK: This girl done lost her goddamn mind.

GERTIE: How did you get out of the house?

CHUCK: Her bedroom window standing wide open. Go look. Go see.

(GERTIE *goes to* ROBBIE's *bedroom.)*

ROBBIE: Let go of me.

(ROBBIE *pulls away from* CHUCK. *He pulls her back.)*

CHUCK: Don't you pull away from me like that. Out here causing trouble. Guess that time in jail didn't teach you a damn thing.

(GERTIE *comes back into the living room.)*

CHUCK: Tell your mother what you did.

(ROBBIE *is silent.)*

CHUCK: Speak.

ROBBIE: I saw those boys going over to Medgar Evers house. So I went to see what they were up to.

CHUCK: So she opened the window. Climbed her narrow ass out the damn house and went after those white boys. I saw the whole thing from my front yard. Then guess what she did.

GERTIE: What did you do?

ROBBIE: I—stood in front of their car—and I stared them down.

CLAUDETTE: Oh my God!

ROBBIE: They called me a nigger.

GERTIE: Robbie!

ROBBIE: Well that's what they called me.

CHUCK: Then she slammed her hand down on the front of the car. Got her blood all over it. Wiped her bloody hand all over the hood.

GERTIE: Blood?

CHUCK: Surprised they didn't run her down after that shit. But they saw me coming from across the street. That's probably what saved your tail.

GERTIE: Blood? What blood?

CHUCK: Show your mama your hand.

(ROBBIE *doesn't comply.*)

CHUCK: What I say?

(ROBBIE *releases her fist. Revealing blood coming from a cut in her hand*)

CHUCK: Show your other hand.

(ROBBIE *shows the other palm with a long ugly scar from a childhood injury.*)

CHUCK: Got herself a matching pair, now. Cut it getting out the house, I suppose.

GERTIE: Let mama see your hand.

(CHUCK *takes the shotgun from* GERTIE *and goes to look out the window.* GERTIE *attends to* ROBBIE.)

GERTIE: Claudette, please baby. I'm counting on you.

CLAUDETTE: Mama, I'm not starting my new life with a troublemaker.

ROBBIE: I don't want to go to California. I want to stay in Jackson.

GERTIE: Did I ask you what you want?

CLAUDETTE: Well about what I want? What about me?

(CLAUDETTE *gathers her things and goes to the door. But* CHUCK *gestures her away.)*

CHUCK: Y'all go in the bedroom and hide.

GERTIE: What's wrong?

CHUCK: Them boys. They parked outside the house.

GERTIE: This house? Our house?

CHUCK: Yeah. Your house. Go!

(GERTIE *and* CLAUDETTE *move toward the bedrooms.* CHUCK *keeps watch at the window.* ROBBIE *stays put.)*

GERTIE: Robbie!

(ROBBIE *shakes her head "no". Refusing to move)*

CHUCK: Fine. She wants to stay. Let her stay. She thinks she big and bad enough.

(GERTIE *and* CLAUDETTE *leave the room.)*

CHUCK: You ever hold a gun?

ROBBIE: No. I don't want to neither. Besides. I don't need it for those boys outside. They were cowards. I could see it in their eyes.

CHUCK: Cowards are the most dangerous kind of crackers there is. Your daddy ain't taught you that yet?

ROBBIE: No sir. He hasn't got around to it yet, I guess.

CHUCK: Then I need to have a word with him.
(Beat)
And speak of the devil.

ROBBIE: Are the white boys still outside too?

CHUCK: Nope. Just your daddy pulling up.
(He quietly watches out the window to make sure everything is safe. Then he sees the boys again.)
Goddamn. Here they come again.

(ROBBIE *runs over and finds a spot in the window to see.*)

ROBBIE: Why they stopping?

CHUCK: Why you think? You stay right here. Guard the door.

(CHUCK *goes outside.* ROBBIE *peeks out the small window in the door. Tense silence for a moment. Then a car horn honks several times. Two shots from a shotgun is heard.* GERTIE *and* CLAUDETTE *come running out of the bedroom.*)

GERTIE: What happened?

(ROBBIE *jumps out of the way of the door as* CHUCK *and* ROBERT-EARL *run in.* CLAUDETTE *runs to* ROBERT-EARL *and wraps her arms around him.* CHUCK *stands by the door just to be safe.*)

CLAUDETTE: Daddy!

ROBERT-EARL: Daddy alright.

GERTIE: Robbie went outside and tried to be John Wayne, trying to intimidate the boys. She could have gotten herself killed.

CLAUDETTE: Could've got all of us killed. And I warned you this would happen. You and Daddy. When she started begging to go down to those Bible Study meetings at the little storefront on Farish.

(ROBERT-EARL *goes to the window and looks out.*)

CLAUDETTE: I told you that wasn't a church. It was N-A-A-C-P youth rallies made to look like church. But nobody listens to a word I say.

ROBERT-EARL:	CLAUDETTE:
Pruitt, you think they're coming back?	I'd heard things. Bad things.
Shit. How long they been outside?	Are you listening to me?

ROBERT-EARL: Claudette, ain't got time right now.

CLAUDETTE: *(Throws her hands in the air)* See!

*(*ROBERT-EARL *picks up the telephone. He dials.)*

ROBERT-EARL: Miss Lottie, Robert-Earl, how you doing.... Ah yeah, yeah these white boys acting the fool. Ain't nothing new. But we got it handled. I was wondering if I could ask a favor...mind if Gertie and the girls come next door and sit with you for a spell.... I appreciate ya.... Yes ma'am. Yes ma'am. Alright, alright. Now are the boys home.... Good. Now can you have one of them come out back and meet the women halfway. Thank you kindly. I sho' appreciate ya. Alright now, here they come.... Love ya too, Miss Lottie.

*(*ROBERT-EARL *grabs his shotgun from* CHUCK *and hurries out back through the kitchen with the ladies.)*

*(*CHUCK *is alone.)*

CHUCK: You're welcome, Robert-Earl. I didn't mind in the least putting my life on the line to save Gertie and them girls of yours. Shit. Goddamn, ungrateful ass.

*(*CHUCK *chuckles. Then mid-chuckle. He stops and buries his face in his hands. His whole body betraying the fear he tried so hard to hide.* ROBERT-EARL *comes back in. He locks the door.)*

CHUCK: Monroe, man we need to talk.

ROBERT-EARL: Need a beer first? Cause I sho' need one.

CHUCK: Yeah. That sound real good.

*(*ROBERT-EARL *goes to the kitchen. After a quick spell he comes back with two beers. He give one to* CHUCK. *Then* CHUCK *pulls out a pack of cigarettes and offers* ROBERT-EARL *one. robert-earl accepts. They drink and smoke.)*

ROBERT-EARL: So. What we need to talk about?

CHUCK: Medgar.

ROBERT-EARL: Medgar? What about Medgar?

CHUCK: I say we string the nigger up. Make it look like the Klan did it.

(ROBERT-EARL *laughs, raising his beer in the air.*)

ROBERT-EARL: I'll drink to that

(CHUCK *and* ROBERT-EARL *toast.* CHUCK *laughs...then.*)

CHUCK: You're joking, right?

ROBERT-EARL: Yeah, I'm joking. Shit, you said it. I didn't.

CHUCK: Man don't look at me like that. I was just saying some shit.

ROBERT-EARL: Pruitt, I know you. If you could get away with it. You would.

CHUCK: I wouldn't do no shit like that. But goddamit, we gotta do something. Shit we done tried everything. Offered to buy him out of the neighborhood. Four times. Rejected every offer. Who turns down all that money? You know what he told Anderson? Said maybe Anderson should move if he didn't like being neighbors.

ROBERT-EARL: Said that same shit to me. You remember. Sat his ass right over there.
(Pointing to the sofa)
Ate my food. Enjoyed my hospitality. Then gonna talk to me like I'm a goddamn fool. Messed up our lives. He messed up things bad that night. Shit. I don't even want to think about it know more.

CHUCK: We gotta think about it. We gotta do something.

ROBERT-EARL: I know a couple of white cats who could put a scare in him.

CHUCK: We tried that already. Didn't work.

ROBERT-EARL: I mean really scare him. Get physical. Put a real hurt on him.

CHUCK: I like Franklin's idea better.

ROBERT-EARL: I can't go with Franklin. Can't do that.

CHUCK: Well you got till Thursday to change your tune and I advise you change it soon.

ROBERT-EARL: Why Thursday?

CHUCK: Medgar leaves town Thursday night. Myrlie and the kids will be all alone. Look, I don't like it either but I think it could work.

ROBERT-EARL: I don't beat up on women. Men don't do that.

CHUCK: We're not saying that we would beat her up. Just get rough with her. Shove her around. Tear up the house. Pop the oldest boy across the head a few times. Wave a gun around. Shove it in his face. Just scare the shit out of them.

ROBERT-EARL: A gun? What if it go off?

CHUCK: Man, we ain't gonna have no bullets in the damn gun.

ROBERT-EARL: I'm sure she got a gun. And I'm sure she knows how to use it.

CHUCK: We'd catch her off guard. She'll never have a chance to get to the gun. She'll see us busting in her house with masks on. She won't know what to think?

ROBERT-EARL: Man, we could get arrested behind that shit. And even if we wear masks, she still gonna know we Negros.

CHUCK: That's the point. She's supposed to know that. See up 'till now, they've only been worried about white folks. But if we start getting after them then that's really gonna mess with their heads. And he might be

willing to put up with shit that happens to him, but
if it happens to his wife and kids directly—they ain't
sticking around for too long after that. And you ain't
even got to worry about the police. Franklin knows a
white boy in the police department. A captain. He'll
cover us. He a real good white boy. Man we know it
will work. Listen, Medgar ain't letting up. And the city
ain't letting up. And these crackers sure ain't letting
up. Medgar has to leave this block. It's now or never.

ROBERT-EARL: Don't want my hands dirty like that. I
wanna be able to sleep at night.

CHUCK: Monroe, tell me something. In the last two
weeks, when was the last time you had a good night's
sleep?

(ROBERT-EARL *can't answer.*)

CHUCK: That's what I thought. And it ain't have
nothing to do with no dirty hands.

(*Beat*)

Huh, how well you sleep that night when that bomb
went off on Medgar's porch?

(*Beat*)

Monroe, you wanna know some shit? Can I talk to you
about some real shit?

ROBERT-EARL: Talk to me.

CHUCK: Monroe, this is just between me and you. Man,
I'm afraid. I'm really afraid. This morning two white
boys from the sheriff's department came by my café.

ROBERT-EARL: What happened?

CHUCK: They came in with a German Shepherd. They
come in from time to time. But this time they came in
with that big ass dog. I said I don't allow animals in my
establishment. They just looked at me like I ain't say
shit. Then they ordered biscuits and gravy. Sat there
for almost two hours didn't touch a bite of food. And

that goddamn German Shepherd growled and barked at everybody that walked in the door. Folks see that big angry dog they turn around and walk away. Shit, that dog jumped up on one lady. She afraid of dogs. She saw that German Shepherd and got all nervous. Set that dog off. Lost all my morning business. Then before they left they called me out of the kitchen. Asked me if Medgar eats at my café? I said "No. That nigger ain't welcome here." Then they asked how my wife was. Said they missed seeing her the last few days. I said she hadn't been feeling well. Then they paid their bill and left. I look down at the receipt and do you know what they wrote?

ROBERT-EARL: What?

CHUCK: My sister-in-law's address.

(ROBERT-EARL *gives* CHUCK *a blank look.*)

CHUCK: Get it?

ROBERT-EARL: I really don't.

CHUCK: I sent my wife to her sister's after they gutted our dog and left her on our doorstep. The note they left me was that they know where my wife is staying. They know our business.

(*Beat*)

How can you forget some shit like that? About me having to send Joanie away. Like you don't even care.

ROBERT-EARL: Pruitt, look it— Man I got a lot on my mind. We all do. We all going through.

CHUCK: Well I'm ready to put this shit to rest and get Medgar off our block once and for all. That's what these crackers want. That's what I want. That's what you want. And Monroe, nigger I ain't pulling no more punches. It is in your best interest to get on board with any and all efforts to get Medgar Evers off our block. Now Robbie done put you in a bad spot and some of the guys feel you can't be trusted. So you need to do whatever it takes to prove your loyalty to the guys. To the neighborhood.

(There is a knock at the door. CHUCK *and* ROBERT-EARL *get quiet.* ROBERT-EARL *picks up the rifle and goes to the door.)*

ROBERT-EARL: Who is it?

JIMMIE: *(From outside)* Dad it's me.

CHUCK: Why ain't that boy got a special knock? I got a special knock. Shit, he need one, too.

*(*ROBERT-EARL *opens the door.* JIMMIE *comes in.)*

ROBERT-EARL: Jimmie. Son.

CHUCK: Professor.

JIMMIE: Mr Chuck. How you?

*(*ROBERT-EARL, *still holding the shotgun, goes to the window and looks out.)*

CHUCK: Just leaving. But…uh…I been meaning to ask. How things going down there at Tougaloo?

JIMMIE: Settling down. Students leaving for the summer.

CHUCK: You know that's not what I meant.

JIMMIE: Faculty is not allowed to get involved in the protests, sir.

CHUCK: Don't matter no way. I suppose. You'll be leaving us soon. When you and Claudette headed to California?

JIMMIE: A few days.

CHUCK: What part?

JIMMIE: Oakland. My hometown.

CHUCK: Never heard of it.
(Beat)

Monroe. Remember what we talked about? Counting on ya.

(CHUCK *leaves.* ROBERT-EARL *closes and locks the door.)*

JIMMIE: I can't wait to get back home. I'm not accustomed to this. People meeting you at front door with guns. It's like a war zone. Jackson is too much for me. I just wanna get back home to Oakland. Where it's nice and peaceful and quiet. And Mr Chuck always gives me a look like he wants to punch me. I don't understand Negros here.

ROBERT-EARL: Awwwwww. His bark is worse than his bite.

JIMMIE: If you say so. Anyway, I went by the house but Claudette wasn't there. *(Stares at the shotgun)* I thought she might...be...here.
What's with the gun? What happened?

(ROBERT-EARL *puts the shotgun down by the window.)*

ROBERT-EARL: I sent Gertie and the girls next door to Miss Lottie's. We had some trouble a little while ago.

JIMMIE: What kind of trouble?

ROBERT-EARL: Don't worry about it. It's over.

(JIMMIE *gives* ROBERT-EARL *a concerned look.)*

ROBERT-EARL: I said don't worry about it.

JIMMIE: Well Dad, it's kind of a good thing that we're alone. There's something important I need to talk to you about.

ROBERT-EARL: I'm listening.

JIMMIE: It's about mother and Robbie. Now you know I love them dearly. And I'd do anything for them and I don't know what your opinion on this is but I don't feel that it is appropriate for Robbie to spend the summer with me and Claudette in California.

ROBERT-EARL: Excuse me?

JIMMIE: Dad. I don't want you to be mad at me. But please hear me out.

ROBERT-EARL: Robbie ain't going to California. What the hell you talking about?

JIMMIE: Mother hasn't said anything to you?

ROBERT-EARL: This is the first I'm hearing about Robbie and California.

JIMMIE: How do you feel about that?

ROBERT-EARL: About the fact that my wife is doing shit behind my back? Or about my baby girl moving across country?

JIMMIE: Both.

ROBERT-EARL: Well you ain't got a damn thing to worry about. Because Robbie is staying right here in Jackson, Mississippi.

JIMMIE: I agree with your decision and I truly think it is for the best.

ROBERT-EARL: Hell yeah it's for the best.

(There is a ruckus from out back. GERTIE, ROBBIE *and* CLAUDETTE *are arguing.)*

JIMMIE: Oh God, here she comes. Please don't tell mother I told you. I thought you knew. I don't want her to be upset with me.

ROBERT-EARL: Too late for that.

JIMMIE: Please don't say anything. Promise me—

(The women come into the living room from the kitchen. ROBBIE's *hand is wrapped in a kitchen towel.)*

CLAUDETTE: What kind of bird don't fly?
(Beat)
A jailbird.

ROBBIE: Leave me alone!

(CLAUDETTE *gets in her sister's face.*)

CLAUDETTE: JAILBIRD!

(GERTIE *pulls* CLAUDETTE *and* ROBBIE *apart.*)

GERTIE: Stop it!
I don't know what I did to deserve such ungrateful children.

CLAUDETTE: We wouldn't be arguing if it wasn't for that one. Jimmie, take me home. Now! I don't want to spend one more minute in this house.

GERTIE: You better watch that tone. You still a child as far as I'm concerned.
(To ROBBIE*)*
And you go to bathroom so I can look after that hand 'fore we take you the doctor.

(ROBBIE *doesn't move. She is quiet. She just stares at her hand.*)

ROBERT-EARL: Gertie, I need to talk to you.

GERTIE: Robert-Earl, you better talk some sense into to these girls.

ROBERT-EARL:	CLAUDETTE:
Who I need to talk to is you—	Jimmie, I said take me home.

GERTIE: I need your support. Why are you giving me two-for-one, Robert-Earl?

ROBERT-EARL: I don't care about that. We got other business.

GERTIE: What business?

CLAUDETTE:	ROBERT-EARL:
Take me home.	Gertie we need to talk.

(CLAUDETTE *shakes her head in frustration and marches off to the door.* JIMMIE *follows. But before she can touch the door, a horrifying sound like a round of gunfire pierces the sky outside. A car speeds off. Followed by another round of gunfire.* CLAUDETTE *jumps back into Jimmie's arms.* GERTIE *covers her ears.*)

ROBERT-EARL: Get down! Get down!

(CLAUDETTE *and* GERTIE *get down on the floor. But* ROBBIE *doesn't move. She stares at the palms of her hand. Blood is coming through the kitchen towel.*)

GERTIE: Robbie?

ROBBIE: It won't stop bleeding. It won't. Stop. *(She passes out. She hits the floor.)*

GERTIE: ROBBIE!!!

(Abrupt black-out)

(End of scene)

Scene Two

(Later that evening. Sometime around eleven)

(The living room is dark. Illuminated only by a lamp light by the sofa and light from the kitchen. ROBERT-EARL *sits in a chair by the sofa. He is awake. He holds his shotgun in his lap. The phone is ringing. He stares at the phone. He doesn't answer.)*

*(*ROBBIE *is sleep on the sofa. She still wears the same clothes from earlier in the day. Her hand is bandaged.)*

(After a moment, GERTIE *comes out. Dressed for bed. She holds a gold lamé cigarette case.)*

(The phone stops ringing.)

GERTIE: How can she sleep through that phone? I can't.

(ROBERT-EARL *doesn't answer*)

GERTIE: Robert-Earl, just let the child go to her room. You can't eyeball her twenty-four seven.

(ROBERT-EARL doesn't answer)

GERTIE: She sleeping ready-rose on the sofa. That ain't good for her.

(Still nothing from ROBERT-EARL)

GERTIE: You still not talking to me?

ROBERT-EARL: She says she doesn't like her bedroom. It's too small. She can't breathe.

GERTIE: She'll be fine. Let me put her to bed. *(She goes to wake ROBBIE.)*

ROBERT-EARL: Don't touch her. Let her sleep.

GERTIE: We boarded up the window. She ain't going nowhere.

ROBERT-EARL: Say she can't breathe.

GERTIE: She'll sleep better in her own bed.
(Reaching her hand out to touch ROBBIE)
Robbie.
She'll sleep better in her own bed.

ROBERT-EARL: What I say?

(GERTIE stops.)

ROBERT-EARL: Go to bed.

(GERTIE doesn't move.)

ROBERT-EARL: Do what I say.

(GERTIE hesitates, then turns to go back to bed. But she gets to the hallway entrance and stops. She lingers.)

GERTIE: I'd sleep better with you in bed next to me. I wake up at night and you're gone. Sitting out here with that gun. Seems like you spend more time with that gun than me. I lie there in the bed alone in the dark.

And I can't go back to sleep. I catch the little I can, but
it ain't much.

(Beat)

I ain't slept right since they killed Chuck and Joanie's
dog. Every time I close my eyes I'm back standing on
that doorstep, seeing poor Lucy with her insides out.
Guts and Blood…blood everywhere. Joanie said one
night they started getting harassing phone calls. Got
phone calls all night long. The next day, Lucy was
dead.

(The phone rings again, startling GERTIE. ROBERT-EARL
doesn't flinch)

GERTIE: Why don't you answer the phone?

ROBERT-EARL: Why don't you go back to bed?

GERTIE: I can't because of the phone.

(Beat)

It makes me sick when the phone rings and you don't
answer it. Just answer the phone.

ROBERT-EARL: I answered it once already.

GERTIE: And what did they say?

ROBERT-EARL: None of your business.

GERTIE: Robert-Earl—

ROBERT-EARL: You ain't the only one got secrets.

*(*GERTIE *attempts to answer the phone)*

ROBERT-EARL: Don't touch the goddamn phone.

*(*GERTIE *stops.)*

GERTIE: You're still mad at me about California, aren't
you?

(She goes to the kitchen table and sits to smoke.)

I need a cigarette.

*(Lights a cigarette. Takes a long drag. Exhales. Watches the
smoke)*

I don't know how many other ways I can apologize.

ROBERT-EARL: You went behind my back.

GERTIE: No, Robert-Earl. I was just trying to get all the pieces lined up before I—

(The phone stops ringing.)

ROBERT-EARL: Claudette and Jimmie leave town Thursday. Today Tuesday. When were you goin' tell me?

(GERTIE doesn't answer)

ROBERT-EARL: Well?

GERTIE: After I convinced Claudette—

ROBERT-EARL: Why didn't you tell me about the bruises on Robbie's back?

(GERTIE gives ROBERT-EARL a guilty look.)

ROBERT-EARL: Yeah I know about the bruises. Miss Lottie called. Asked how they was healing. Why she know and I don't?

GERTIE: Miss Lottie used to be a nurse.
(Beat)
The color is changing. They're getting better. It's not as bad as it sounds.

ROBERT-EARL: That's not what I asked you. I want to see these bruises for myself.
(Gently shakes ROBBIE)
Robbie…Robbie…

GERTIE: Just let her sleep. You can see them in the morning.

ROBERT-EARL: No. I want to see now.
(He turns on the lights and turns off the lamp. And begins to shake ROBBIE)
Wake up. Robbie…Robbie…

(GERTIE *tries to stop* ROBERT-EARL *but he shakes her off and goes back to waking* ROBBIE. *She hard to wake. He shakes her harder.*)

GERTIE:	ROBERT-EARL:
Robert-Earl. You're not making sense. First you want her to sleep. Now you're waking her up. You're not making sense. You're tired. You haven't been to bed since last night. Robert-Earl—	Robbie...ROBERTA! Wake-up. Daddy wanna see them bruises on your back. I wanna see.

(ROBBIE *wakes.*)

ROBERT-EARL: Show me those bruises, baby. Show me.

GERTIE: Robert-Earl, she has to take off—

ROBERT-EARL: I don't care.

GERTIE: Well I do—

ROBERT-EARL: Roberta, show me the bruises. Now.

GERTIE: Let me take her in the bathroom at least... Get her undressed and I'll call you in. I don't likeit out in the living room like this. Baby, come on let's go to the bathroom.

(GERTIE *and* ROBBIE *gets up to go to the bathroom.*)

ROBERT-EARL: Gertie... How big are the bruises?

GERTIE: You'll see.

(*The phone rings.* GERTIE *and* ROBBIE *stop.*)

ROBERT-EARL: Go to the bathroom.

GERTIE: You going to answer that?

ROBERT-EARL: Go to the bathroom first. Go.

(GERTIE *and* ROBBIE *go.* ROBERT-EARL *hesitates. Then he answers the phone.*)

ROBERT-EARL: Hello. *(Beat. Slow burn)* You burn in hell.

(ROBERT-EARL hangs up the phone. He gets his gun
then goes to the window and looks out. After a beat,
the phone rings again. He lets it ring a few times before
he picks it up. But instead of answering he pushes the
button, disconnecting the call. He doesn'thang the
phone up so that no more calls can come through. The
there is a knock at the door. He is startled.

JIMMIE: *(From outside)* Mom. Dad. It's me…. Hello…

(ROBERT-EARL *opens the door.* JIMMIE *comes in.* ROBERT-
EARL *closes the door.)*

JIMMIE: Thank God. I was hoping somebody was up.

ROBERT-EARL: Boy, what is your damn problem?
It'safter midnight.

JIMMIE: We got into a bad argument and Claudette has
locked me out of the house. I need mother to come and
talk some sense into her and make her open the door.

ROBERT-EARL: Why Gertie?

JIMMIE: Claudette is exhibiting highly irrational female
behavior. I think another male voice might set her off
again.

ROBERT-EARL: Gertie ain't going out this time of night.

JIMMIE: Can you drive her?

ROBERT-EARL: Go home. Knock on the damn door and
tell Claudette to call her mama.

JIMMIE: Dad, Claudette can't call. She broke the phone.

ROBERT-EARL: How she break the phone?

JIMMIE: She threw it at the wall.

ROBERT-EARL: Why she throw the phone at the wall?

JIMMIE: Irrational female behavior. Like I said. No
rhyme or reason. She's been acting real strange.

ROBERT-EARL: Women don't throw phones for no reason. You got to give them a reason.

JIMMIE: Dad, it's psychological.

ROBERT-EARL: You saying Claudette crazy?

JIMMIE: No sir.

ROBERT-EARL: Then why she throw the phone?

GERTIE: *(O S)* Robert-Earl. Robert-Earl. We're ready.

JIMMIE: *(Calling out)* Mother. Mother, I need to see you.

ROBERT-EARL: Gertie ain't going nowhere this time of night.

(GERTIE comes out.)

GERTIE: Jimmie? What's wrong? Where's Claudette?

JIMMIE: She locked me out of the house. We had a fight?

GERTIE: A fight about what?

JIMMIE: I don't know. She's just been acting real short with me lately. And when I finally said something about her ugliness towards me, she explodes. I've never seen her act this way.

(A pounding noise is heard. Coming from the bathroom)

ROBERT-EARL: What the hell is that?

(More pounding.)

(ROBBIE comes running into the room. She wears only her bra and panties. Panting for air)

GERTIE: Robbie!

(GERTIE goes and throws her arms around ROBBIE to shield her.)

ROBBIE: I couldn't breathe. It was too small. I couldn't breathe. It was too small.

(GERTIE rushes ROBBIE to the bathroom.)

GERTIE: Jimmie, don't go. I need to talk to you and Robert-Earl. Together. Stay.

JIMMIE: I can't take Robbie to California like that. I know that's what mother wants to talk about.

ROBERT-EARL: Anybody think I'm going to let Robbie go to California done lost their damn mind.

JIMMIE: Claudette is against the idea too. Dad, you have my support.

ROBERT-EARL: I don't need your support. This my house.

JIMMIE: I know that. But my point is that—

(GERTIE *comes into the room.*)

GERTIE: Just one month. Four weeks is all I ask. It doesn't have to be for the whole summer. Just let Robbie go to California for one month.

ROBERT-EARL: Gertie, I said no.

GERTIE: You said no to the whole summer. I'mjust asking for a few weeks.
(*To* JIMMIE)
Son. Listen to me. It'll be good to have her with you.

ROBERT-EARL: Gertie!

GERTIE: I'm talking to Jimmie— It'll be good. Robbie can help Claudette get settled and she can keep her from getting too homesick. If she starts getting homesick then there will just be problems all the time—

JIMMIE: But if you and dad are not in agree—

GERTIE: And See. See. That's the reason Claudette is giving you so much blues right now. Because she already getting homesick. A mother knows these things.

ROBERT-EARL: She needs to be home where we can look after her. Robbie, ain't been right since she got out of jail. She's not acting in her right mind—

GERTIE: Then just two weeks. Just a little vacation. Some time to get her mind straight. Jimmie, listen—

ROBERT-EARL: Jimmie ain't running a damn thing in this house, If I say Robbie ain't going, then Robbie—

JIMMIE: Look, I'm not trying to cause trouble, but—

GERTIE: Goddamn!

(That got JIMMIE's *and* ROBERT-EARL's *attention.)*

GERTIE: Will somebody listen to me? Robbie needs to leave Jackson. Soon. Period. Something very bad is going to happen. And I don't want Robbie here when it happens.

ROBERT-EARL: How soon?

GERTIE: Soon. That's all I know.

ROBERT-EARL: I think you know more.

GERTIE: All I know is soon. And I pray that don't mean before Thursday.

ROBERT-EARL: Tell me what's supposed to happen first.

GERTIE: I don't know. All I know is something bad. That's all I heard.

ROBERT-EARL: Who you hear it from?

*(*JIMMIE *puts two and two together.)*

JIMMIE: Well I'll be damned.
(He stares at his in-laws in disbelief.)

ROBERT-EARL: Jimmie go home.

*(*JIMMIE *stays put.* ROBERT-EARL *cuts his eyes at* JIMMIE*)*

ROBERT-EARL: You hear me, boy?

(JIMMIE *storms out. Slamming the door)*

ROBERT-EARL: Tell me everything you know. I don't want no more surprises.

(A moment passes between ROBERT-EARL *and* GERTIE *before she speaks.)*

GERTIE: I would never intentionally do anything to hurt you. But sometimes I just don't have a choice. You know— The world keeps changing Robert-Earl. We have to change with it. Means we have to do things we don't want to do. Let our children go. Put the phone back on the hook. What's meant to happen will happen. There's nothing we can do to stop it. We have to face what's facing us. We have to find a way to survive. And Robbie needs to leave Mississippi. No ifs, ands, buts about it. That's all I can say on that.
(She puts the phone back on the hook.)

(The phone rings.)

(End of scene)

Scene Three

(Around eleven the next morning. ROBBIE *sits at the dinner table. Her breakfast—cereal and orange juice—sits in front of her. But she hasn't touched it. She just gives* CLAUDETTE *the annoying kid sister stare.* CLAUDETTE *is on the phone.)*

CLAUDETTE: It's a family heirloom. I can't sell that. It goes back to mama. No ma'am. You are mistaken. I never promised that—
(Notices ROBBIE*)*
Hold one moment Cloreatha.
(Beat)
Roberta Gertrude Monroe. What is your problem?

ROBBIE: Mama said you supposed to be watching me while she and daddy at work.

CLAUDETTE: You are sixteen years old. You do not need watching after.

ROBBIE: I might run away.

CLAUDETTE: Then run. I'll help you pack.
Girl, please. I got business.
(Back on the phone)
Cloreatha I'm back....
Picking furniture isn't Donald Ray's job. That's your job. You're the wife.... Well if you find out in the next hour call me back at my mama's house.... Alright girl, bye.

(CLAUDETTE hangs up the phone and looks back at ROBBIE who is still staring at her.)

ROBBIE: We're not supposed to answer the phone. Remember? Only daddy can answer the phone from now on. So what you gonna do if she calls you back?

CLAUDETTE: Dammit. You let me worry about that. That's my business. Can't even answer the damn telephone. I can't wait to get out of Mississippi.
(Beat)
And stop staring at me and eat your breakfast.

ROBBIE: I'm not eating it. I've decided to go on a hunger strike.

CLAUDETTE: A what? Hunger Strike?
Girl, please. You don't half eat, anyway.

ROBBIE: Well now I'm making it official and I'm not eating until my demands are met.

CLAUDETTE: What demands?

ROBBIE: To be let off punishment and to be able to participate in the protests again and that mom and dad invite Medgar Evers and his family over for dinner so that they can see—

(CLAUDETTE *begins to laugh.* ROBBIE *talks over her laughter.*)

ROBBIE: —that he is not the bad guy they make him out to be.

CLAUDETTE: We had him over for dinner. Don't you remember what happened?

ROBBIE: That was a long time ago.

CLAUDETTE: It wasn't that long.

ROBBIE: It was too. I was twelve years old.

CLAUDETTE: That's only four years ago.

ROBBIE: A lot can change in four years. And people can change. For the better. And you weren't even here that night. It was right before you—

CLAUDETTE: That wasn't my fault. I didn't do anything wrong. And why you have to bring that up for?

ROBBIE: What? Oh…sorry.

(Beat)

But I didn't mean—

CLAUDETTE: *(Waving her hand in* ROBBIE's *face)* All that matters is that I'm right and you're wrong. And anyway, mama said after what happened that night the Evers came over, there ain't no way in hell Medgar Evers would ever step foot back in this house. And beyond that, don't you remember Mr Eubie Proctor? He had Medgar over for dinner and the very next day his paint and body shop was set on fire. That was just six months ago.

ROBBIE: And that was because he had Medgar Evers over for dinner?

CLAUDETTE: Why else?

ROBBIE: It could be anything.

(Beat)

Okay so what you're telling me is that some random, roving crackers just happened to be sitting outside Mr Proctor's house of all the houses in the neighborhood. Saw Medgar go over for dinner and just happened to know that Mr Proctor has a paint and body shop and where it's located and set fire to the place. That's what you telling me?

CLAUDETTE: No. What I'm telling you is that this neighborhood has a lot of eyes and ears and those eyes and ears are Negro and what they see and hear they report back to white folks.

ROBBIE: What White folks?

CLAUDETTE: The White Citizens Council. The Mississippi Sovereignty Commission. The Klan. The police. It doesn't matter. Pick your poison. It's all the same thing.

ROBBIE: Negros report to the Klan?

CLAUDETTE: Some do. Not all. But some do. And some of them live on this very street.

(Beat)

Maybe even in this very house.

ROBBIE: Take that back.

(CLAUDETTE starts laughing.)

CLAUDETTE: I got you good.

ROBBIE: You were joking?

CLAUDETTE: Yes.

No.

Maybe.

You never know who to trust. You have to be careful.

(CLAUDETTE gives ROBBIE a wicked grin. ROBBIE goes back to the kitchen table and sits. She stares at her food)

CLAUDETTE: That shut you up.

(ROBBIE *stares at the old childhood scar on her palm. She traces it with the index finger of her other hand.* CLAUDETTE *stares at her*)

CLAUDETTE: Okay. Now you're too quiet.

ROBBIE: Did you see that they boarded up my bedroom window? Like I live in a prison. Like I'm still in that jail cell.

(Beat)

Don't matter I suppose.

Sometimes I feel like I been living in jail even before I got arrested.

(CLAUDETTE *stares at* ROBBIE.)

(Quiet. Then the phone rings.)

(The phone rings, again. And again.)

(CLAUDETTE *looks at the phone.*)

ROBBIE: I dare you to answer the phone.

(The phone is still ringing)

ROBBIE: You're afraid to answer the phone.

CLAUDETTE: I am not afraid.

(Phone rings.)

ROBBIE: Answer it. Answer it. Answer it. Answer it.

(The phone keeps ringing)

CLAUDETTE: Stop it!

ROBBIE: Answer it. You already said it was a dumb rule. What if it's Cloretha calling back about the furniture? Girl, you gonna miss your money.

(ROBBIE *laughs.* CLAUDETTE *stares at the phone, tempted to answer but afraid. After a beat, the phone stops ringing.* ROBBIE *laughs more.*)

ROBBIE: Why did you break your phone?

(CLAUDETTE *doesn't answer.*)

ROBBIE: You can tell me. I might even take your side.

CLAUDETTE: You're not going to take my side.

ROBBIE: How do you know?

CLAUDETTE: Because I'm a blind, deaf and dumb, cog in the wheel of the White oppression of the Negro in America.

ROBBIE: What?

CLAUDETTE: That's what you called me.

ROBBIE: I called you that? When?

CLAUDETTE: When I refused to give you a ride to one of those youth rallies on Farish Street.

ROBBIE: Oh.
(Beat)
I remember now. I was just mad at you. I didn't mean it.
Tell me.
(She closes her eyes. Smiles real bright and shakes her body from side to side)
Pleeeeeeeeeeeeeeeeeaaaaaaasssssssse.

CLAUDETTE: *(Trying not to laugh)* Stop that.

ROBBIE: *(Even cuter this time)*
Pleeeeeeeeeeeeeeeeeaaaaaaasssssssse.

CLAUDETTE: You're not three years old. That doesn't work on me anymore.

ROBBIE: Yes it does.
(If cute could kill....)
Pleeeeeeeeeeeeeeeeeaaaaaaasssssssse.

CLAUDETTE: *(Laughing)* That's not fair.

ROBBIE: (...CLAUDETTE *would be six feet under*)
Pleeeeeeeeeeeeeeeeaaaaaaassssssssse.

CLAUDETTE: Okay. Okay. I give up. I surrender. But if
I tell you then you have to promise not to tell mom or
dad what happened. You promise?

ROBBIE: I promise.

(CLAUDETTE *and* ROBBIE *pinkie swear.*)

CLAUDETTE: Okay now I'm bringing you into my
confidence like big sister little sister.

ROBBIE: I know. I know. Now tell me what happened.

CLAUDETTE: I threw the phone at Myrlie Evers' head
and it broke.

ROBBIE: You did what?

CLAUDETTE: Myrlie Evers came over to our house late
last night and I asked her to leave and she wouldn't
leave—

ROBBIE: So you threw the phone at Myrlie Evers' head?

CLAUDETTE: Well I didn't throw the phone just to be
hateful and throw a phone. I'm not that kind of person.
I threw the phone to stop her from using our phone.
She was trying to use our phone.

ROBBIE: Well what was wrong with her using your
phone?

CLAUDETTE: Well A. She has her own damn phone. But
she was scared to use her phone because she was afraid
her phone was tapped. That is not my problem. And B.
Whatever conversation she was intending to have was
not a conversation that needed to be had on my phone
especially if she was worried about her phone being
tapped.

ROBBIE: She probably just wanted to call Medgar.

CLAUDETTE: No. She said she wanted to call her mother.

ROBBIE: You wouldn't let her talk to her own mother?

CLAUDETTE: See. I knew you wouldn't take my side.

ROBBIE: You chucked a phone at Myrlie Evers' head.

CLAUDETTE: Her head just happened to be in the way. And anyway she ducked.

ROBBIE: Thank God.

(There's a knock at the door.)

JIMMIE: *(O S)* Claudette. It's Jimmie. I know you're in there.

CLAUDETTE: *(Hushed)* I'm not here.

ROBBIE: He already knows you're here.

CLAUDETTE: I don't want to see him.

(More knocking)

CLAUDETTE: I'm still mad at him. I'm not letting him off the hook that easy. I'mhiding in the bathroom. Don't tell him I'm here.

ROBBIE: Well what if he has to use the bathroom?

CLAUDETTE: He can go home and use the bathroom.

(CLAUDETTE runs to the bathroom and slams the door. ROBBIE opens the door. JIMMIE comes in.)

JIMMIE: Where's Claudette?

ROBBIE: Hiding in the bathroom until you leave.

(JIMMIE heads for the bathroom.)

ROBBIE: No point in trying. She's not coming out.

(JIMMIE goes down the hall anyway. Knocking is heard.)

JIMMIE: *(O S)* Claudette…Claudette…Claudette please talk to me.

(More knocking)

This is childish…. Claudette.

(He comes back into the living room.)

ROBBIE: Claudette told me what happened. She threw a phone at Myrlie Evers' head?

JIMMIE: She told you that?

ROBBIE: Is that really what happened?

JIMMIE: *(Hushed)* Are we alone?

ROBBIE: 'Cept for Claudette in the bathroom, yes. Mom and dad at school. Finishing up. Why was Myrlie at your house? Late at night.

JIMMIE: To use the phone.

ROBBIE: Yeah but why your phone? Of all the phones on this street?

JIMMIE: I guess she trust me.

ROBBIE: Why?

JIMMIE: Before I married your sister—

ROBBIE: You had an affair with Myrlie Evers?

JIMMIE: No. Before we were married, when I lived on campus I offered my place as a safe house for Myrlie and the kids if they were ever scared and needed a place to hide. Late at night after folks went to bed Medgar would have someone call me with a secret code and that was my sign to drive over to the house and pick-up the family.

ROBBIE: Jimmie. That makes you a hero.

JIMMIE: Not so much. After I started courting your sister I began to get cold feet because I knew your family wouldn't approve. So I offered to do something else maybe. But Medgar just shut me down. Said I was like all the others. So last night, I was shocked when

Myrlie came to my door. And I couldn't turn her away.
I knew it had to be something important for her to
come to my house after my ending on bad terms with
Medgar.

ROBBIE: And Claudette threw a phone at her head.
That's a damn shame.

JIMMIE: I tried to explain to Claudette what was
happening and that's when she just—
(Yelling toward the bathroom)
LOST HER MIND.

(ROBBIE starts laughing.)

ROBBIE: That sounds just like Claudette. Wanna hear a
funny story? When I was in jail—

(JIMMIE gives ROBBIE a curious look)

ROBBIE: no it gets funny. When I was in jail, there was
this girl, Etta Dean Jackson that reminded me so much
of Claudette I wanted to slap her. And everybody
hated her. The worst part of being in jail was Etta
Dean Jackson. Hand to God. She cried, and carried on,
got on our nerves. Listen to what Etta Dean did. One
night, we had been singing freedom songs and we
wouldn't stop. We sang and sang. So to get us to stop,
some guards came and pulled six girls out and made
them go around the corner. They said they had to do a
search. And then we heard them say "take off all your
clothes." And we all got scared, and we could hear
some of the girls crying as they took off their clothes,
and do you know Etta Dean sat in that corner and
pissed herself. Right next to me. I had to smell that for
the rest of the night. We all did.

JIMMIE: She was scared. I'd be scared too.

ROBBIE: Yeah, but she didn't have to pee on herself.

JIMMIE: That's not funny.

ROBBIE: If you knew Etta Dean it would be funny—

JIMMIE: It wouldn't be funny if it happened to you. Would it?

ROBBIE: You should be strong. Not show any fear. Be a rock. Not back down.

JIMMIE: Says who?

ROBBIE: Says me.
(Beat)
We had this big bucket for drinking water and we had to dip our cup. You know like that—
(She demonstrates.)
—and there was this one guard, he took a real bad disliking to me. I think because I always looked him right in the eye. Like, "I'm not afraid of you." And this one day I was so thirsty and I went to the bucket and he was standing there. And as I went to dip my cup, he hawked and spit right in the water. A big wad of spit. Well I dipped my cup and drank my water anyway, gave him the biggest smile and walked away. I wasn't giving him the satisfaction. If I'm thirsty, I'm thirsty and there's nothing he can do about it.

JIMMIE: What if he shit in the water?

ROBBIE: Well I wouldn't drink that. I'm not crazy. Spit is different than shit.

JIMMIE: There's all kinds of germs in spit.

ROBBIE: I was standing up for myself. My point is that you stand up for yourself and you don't cower. You NEVER cower. You take your licks. I'm gonna earn my pin.
(She taps below her left shoulder.)

JIMMIE: Earn your pin?

ROBBIE: Sho-nuff. I'm gonna earn my pin.

JIMMIE: What does that mean?

ROBBIE: My pin. My badge of honor. I'm gonna earn it.

JIMMIE: Is that how you got those bruises on your back?
Earning your pin?

(ROBBIE *is quiet for a moment*)

JIMMIE: Well?

ROBBIE: Just got knocked around a little.

JIMMIE: Robbie, I don't believe Etta Dean was the worst
thing that happened to you in jail. You haven't been
the same Robbie that I knew before.
(Beat)
You scared me last night.

ROBBIE: I didn't know you were here. I just had trouble
breathing.

JIMMIE: Why do you have trouble breathing?

ROBBIE: Don't know.

JIMMIE: I don't recall you ever having trouble
breathing.

ROBBIE: It'll go away soon. I guess.

JIMMIE: Is it physical as in having trouble with your
lungs and your chest? Or is it just fear?

ROBBIE: I'm not afraid of nothing and nobody.

JIMMIE: Myrlie was afraid when she came to my house
last night. My students are afraid sometimes. Heck
even Medgar is fearful at times. Sometimes fear can
stop you dead in your tracks. Grab your throat and
hold it in the palm of its hand. Everybody is afraid
sometimes. It's okay to be afraid.

ROBBIE: Are you afraid? Is that why you're running
away?

JIMMIE: I'm not running away. But one day I woke up and realized that I'm ready to start a family. And I don't want to raise my children in Mississippi.

ROBBIE: Call it what you want. But it still sounds like running away to me.

JIMMIE: I'm not a coward.

ROBBIE: Did I call you a coward? You chose that word. Not me. So what that say? Huh?

JIMMIE: Fine. When your sister comes out the bathroom, tell her to come home. Can you do that?

(He heads for the door.)

ROBBIE: I know about how you helped the students at Tougaloo. I was always proud of you. I go down to the meetings on Farish and hear good things about you. All the time. And I'dsay to everybody. Jimmie Hollins is my brother. I didn't even say brother-in-law. I said, my brother. My big brother. Folks say, oh there go Jimmie's kid sister. I be proud as a peacock everytime they say that.

(Beat)

I've just been mad that you're leaving. Heartless mad sometimes. We need you. We look up to you. Jimmie, don't go. Stay in Mississippi—and fight.

(JIMMIE doesn't know what to say. CLAUDETTE storms into the living room.)

CLAUDETTE: Jimmie, how long were you intending to let me stay in the bathroom? All damn day, I suppose.

JIMMIE: How long you stay in that bathroom was up to you. Not me.

CLAUDETTE: Don't you care about our marriage?

JIMMIE: We can talk about this at home.

CLAUDETTE: No. I want to talk about this now. Robbie go to your room.

ROBBIE: He already knows I know about Myrlie. So no point in me going to my room.

CLAUDETTE: I told you that in sisterly confidence.

ROBBIE: You said not to tell mom and dad. He ain't mom and dad.

CLAUDETTE: Fine. I'm getting my shit and I'm going home.

(*Grabs her bag then goes to the door. She stops and waits for* JIMMIE)
You coming?

JIMMIE: I'll be there when I feel like it.

CLAUDETTE: Oh. Oh really. Fine then.

(*There is a knock at the door. A special knock.* CLAUDETTE *flinches. Then she opens the door. It's* CHUCK.)

CLAUDETTE: Hello Mr Chuck.

CHUCK: Claudette, how you?

CLAUDETTE: Fine, sir.

CHUCK: Robbie.

ROBBIE: Hi Mr Chuck.

(*Quiet.* JIMMIE *waits to be acknowledged.* CHUCK *gives nothing.*)

JIMMIE: Fine. I'll speak first. How you, sir?

CHUCK: Fine.
(*Beat*)
Claudette, you alright?

(CLAUDETTE *nods her head.*)

CHUCK: You sure about that? You don't look so good.

CLAUDETTE: I'm fine. Thank you for asking.

CHUCK: (*To* JIMMIE) Your wife looks worried about something. Or is it just me?

JIMMIE: Come on Claudette, let's go home.

(The door opens. ROBERT-EARL and GERTIE come inside. GERTIE's face is a mess. She is crying.)

CLAUDETTE: What happened? Mama, why are you crying?

ROBERT-EARL: We got to the school and were told to report immediately to the principal. We've been suspended without pay pending an investigation.

GERTIE: I asked if the investigation will be over before summer school starts. Principal said I won't be teaching summer school. I can't believe this is happening to me. To me. ME.
(She goes to her room.)

ROBBIE: An investigation into what?

CHUCK: Not a damn thing. They're harassing them 'cause of you.

ROBERT-EARL: I saw a piece of paper on the principal's desk. It was a list of names. Your name was on the list.

CLAUDETTE: See, you and mama let Robbie get out of hand. I predicted all of this. Yes I did.

ROBERT-EARL: Well since you know so damn much. You get a chance to prove it.
(Beat)
Gertie! Gertie! Come back out here. Gertie.

(GERTIE comes back out)

ROBERT-EARL: Wipe your face, Gertie. I'm about to make you real happy. Look like you gonna get your wish.

(CLAUDETTE gasps. She knows what is coming next.)

ROBERT-EARL: Claudette. Jimmie. You're taking Robbie to California.

ROBBIE: I don't want to go California.

ROBERT-EARL: I didn't want you to go downtown to the protest. But you went anyway. Didn't give a damn about what I wanted. So now, I don't give a damn what you want.

JIMMIE: Well what about what we want? What if we say no?

GERTIE: Please Jimmie. I'm begging you—

ROBERT-EARL: You ain't gotta beg this boy for a damn thing. As much as we've done to help them get on their feet. Shit, he owe us. They both do—

ROBBIE: I don't want to go—

ROBERT-EARL: That ain't my problem, no more. I wash my hands. I wash my hands of you—

GERTIE: Robert-Earl!

ROBERT-EARL: About to lose our goddamn jobs behind a disobedient, ungrateful—

GERTIE: Robert-Earl, don't talk to her like that—

ROBERT-EARL: The only thing they understand is when you talk to them crazy. Pack your shit and get out of my house. Go stay with your sister and get the hell out of my face. Maybe she'll listen to you because she sho as hell don't listen to me.

JIMMIE: Maybe there is some other family she can stay with.

ROBERT-EARL: Who gave you the deposit to get your place?

JIMMIE: You did.

ROBERT-EARL: Who paid your rent three times when the school messed up your pay?

JIMMIE: You.

ROBERT-EARL: Who bought the car you own cash-money so you wouldn't have to drive around in that piece of shit your s'ditty-ass family from *Oakland, California* sent you down here with?

(JIMMIE *bites his lip. He doesn't answer*)

ROBERT-EARL: Don't bite you lip. Answer the damn question.

JIMMIE: You.

ROBERT-EARL: That's right, goddammit! Gertie and I do everything we can for you. Treat you like our own flesh and blood. Turn a blind eye to that shit you do at Tougaloo. We ain't stupid. We know. Saved your sorry ass—

GERTIE: Robert-Earl, your language. Robert-Earl, the girls.

ROBERT-EARL: They wanna act grown. I'm gonna talk grown. And I don't give a good goddamn who don't like it.

GERTIE: Oh Lord, Jesus. Jesus.

CHUCK: Monroe!

ROBERT-EARL: I'm not talking to you Pruitt. Stay out of it.

(To JIMMIE*)*

I ask you to do one thing.

ROBERT-EARL:	CHUCK:
One thing. One simple thing. And you gonna tell me what you not gonna do—	But Monroe. Monroe!

CHUCK: Dammit *Robert-Earl*! Listen to me. There's something you need to know before you send your girls off with that boy.

ROBERT-EARL: What? What Pruitt? What's so damn important?

CHUCK: I didn't want you to find out this way but Myrlie Evers was over at their house late last night.

ROBERT-EARL: Claudette, you know anything about this?

CHUCK: It could very innocent. She could be going over to borrow some sugar, at eleven o'clock at night.

GERTIE: Claudette? Jimmie?

ROBERT-EARL: What happened last night?

CHUCK: Oh they had a knock down drag out. I'm told. W J said they were so loud he could hear the whole thing from his bedroom window. Said it sounded like one of those—somebody got caught with their pants all the way down knock down drag outs—if you know what I mean.

ROBERT-EARL: Y'all did fight last night. That's what the fight was about? It was about a woman.

CHUCK: And not just any woman. Myrlie—the second worst thing that ever happened to this neighborhood— Evers.

GERTIE: Jimmie. Tell me it's not true.

JIMMIE: I don't know what he's talking about.

CHUCK: Truth will come out one way or the other. Ain't no use in lying. Man just come out and admit you fooled around with Myrlie Evers.

ROBERT-EARL: Jimmie, you been fucking around on my daughter?

JIMMIE: I love her and I would never do anything to hurt Claudette.

CHUCK: He's a lie. Shit, look at the expression on Claudette's face. Look at her eyes. The eyes tell everything.

ROBERT-EARL: Claudette, look me in the eyes. Is what he saying the truth? Myrlie come over to your house last night?

CLAUDETTE: Yes, sir. But—

ROBERT-EARL: *(To* JIMMIE*)* Why didn't you say nothing about Myrlie Evers last night?

*(*JIMMIE *doesn't know how to answer)*

ROBERT-EARL: Goddamn.

CHUCK: And just think. He did all this shit right up under your nose. Imagine how he'll treat your girls when he gets them all the way out in California. Alone.

ROBERT-EARL: I'll kill you.

*(*ROBERT-EARL *charges toward* JIMMIE. CLAUDETTE *and* GERTIE *scream.* ROBBIE *jumps between* ROBERT-EARL *and* JIMMIE.*)*

ROBBIE: Daddy. It's not what you think. Calm down.

*(*JIMMIE *shakes his head at* ROBBIE, *urging her not to say anything.)*

ROBBIE: You want him to kill you instead? Daddy, Jimmie isn't having an affair with Myrlie Evers.

GERTIE: What do you know about this?

ROBBIE: He told me. He used to be a safe-house for Myrlie and the kids when Medgar was out of town. Myrlie came to his house last night because she just needed help and he was trying to help her. That's all.

GERTIE: Is that true?

JIMMIE: I couldn't turn her away.

CHUCK: Nigger, it would be better if you had been fucking her.

(End of scene)

Scene Four

(Wednesday. A little after midnight)

(The shotgun sits by the door.)

(ROBERT-EARL and CHUCK pace the floor. They look worried. The phone rings. ROBERT-EARL races to answer it. But CHUCK beats him to it. CHUCK places his hand over the phone.

CHUCK: Robert-Earl, just let me handle it. Okay? Just sit down for a spell. You making me nervous.

(He answers the phone.)

(ROBERT-EARL sits.)

CHUCK: Hello—
May I ask who's calling—
Hello—
Hello—
(He hangs up the phone.)

ROBERT-EARL: What happened?

CHUCK: It was that lady that called about five minutes ago. She asked for Gertie then she hung up.

ROBERT-EARL: Negro lady or white lady?

CHUCK: I couldn't tell.

(ROBERT-EARL jumps back up and begins pacing again.)

ROBERT-EARL: Where is Gertie? Where is my wife?

CHUCK: Dammit Robert-Earl. Just stop all this shit. Now you got me worried. Gertie coming from church. Tuesday night choir rehearsal. This ain't nothing new. The ladies always come home late on Tuesdays.

ROBERT-EARL: Gertie ain't ever been this late getting home.

CHUCK: Maybe she just sore 'cause of how you talked today. Maybe she just driving around.

ROBERT-EARL: Gertie wouldn't do nothing like that.
A Negro woman just driving around Jackson at
midnight. She know better than that.
(Beat)
What if this has something to do with Robbie's name
being on that list? What if it has something to do with
Jimmie and Myrlie Evers?
(Beat)
Pruitt, I been thinking about Franklin's idea.

CHUCK: Yeah?

ROBERT-EARL: I can't hit Myrlie. Rough up her or
nothing like that. I can't—
But maybe—
I can be a look-out.
I can break shit.
I can call her all kinds of horrible names.
I can do that.
(Beat)
We'll wear masks? Right?

CHUCK: Right.

(ROBERT-EARL covers his face.)

CHUCK: What's wrong?

ROBERT-EARL: I'm getting light-headed.

CHUCK: *(Sits his friend down at the dining table)* Sit down.
Relax. It's gonna be alright.

(The phone rings again. CHUCK answers.)

CHUCK: Hello—
Miss, did you just call a minute ago—

ROBERT-EARL: *(Takes the phone out of CHUCK's hand)*
Who is this? What do you want with my wife?
Hello—
Hello—

Goddamit.

(ROBERT-EARL *hangs up the phone. The door unlocks.*
GERTIE *comes in.*)

ROBERT-EARL: Where the hell have you been?

GERTIE: At church. You know where I've been.

ROBERT-EARL: Since when choir rehearsal let out after midnight?

GERTIE: The roads blocked.

CHUCK: Blocked?

GERTIE: Up the street. Somebody put some mess in the road. Can't get by. One way in. One way out.

ROBERT-EARL: Took you two hours to get around a road block?

GERTIE: After choir rehearsals we sat in the sanctuary and had a meeting about folks being let off

their jobs.

CHUCK: A N-A-A-C-P meeting?

GERTIE: Yes.
(Beat)
I just sat and listened like I always do. I didn't say nothing.

ROBERT-EARL: Girl, I been scared out my mind, worried about you. And some woman keep calling for you. I didn't know what to think.

GERTIE: What woman?

ROBERT-EARL: I don't know. Didn't give a name. Just kept hanging up?

GERTIE: A white woman?

(GERTIE *runs to the phone.* ROBERT-EARL *slams his hand down on it to stop her from using it.*)

ROBERT-EARL: What is going on?

GERTIE: Robert-Earl. I need to use the phone. Now.

ROBERT-EARL: Tell me what's going on.

GERTIE: Robert-Earl, I need to use the phone. I need some privacy.

ROBERT-EARL: Privacy for what?

GERTIE: Stop giving me two for one. Let me use the phone.

(There is banging at the door. Everyone jumps.)

CLAUDETTE: *(O S)* Mama! Daddy!

GERTIE: Claudette!

(CHUCK opens the front door. CLAUDETTE is in night attire and barefoot. She is crying. She runs into GERTIE's arms and sobs.)

GERTIE: Baby!

CHUCK: Girl, what you doing outside this time of night?

GERTIE: Baby, what's wrong? What happened? Where's Jimmie?

CLAUDETTE: He kicked me out of the house.

ROBERT-EARL: He what?

CLAUDETTE: We started fighting again and he told me to leave. He cussed me. He said to get out of his goddamn house. Why would he say that to me?

(She breaks down again.)

ROBERT-EARL: *(Rushing to the door)* Sonofabitch gonna die.

GERTIE: *(Still holding CLAUDETTE)* No Robert-Earl. No. No. Chuck, stop him.

(CHUCK jumps in front of the door and blocks it.)

ROBERT-EARL: Get out of my way Chuck. Get out of my way. I'll hurt you too if you don't get out of my way.

CHUCK: Man just calm down. Calm down.

ROBERT-EARL: I don't wanna calm down.

(There is a knock at the door.)

JIMMIE: *(O S)* It's me. Is Claudette here? I've come to apologize.

(CLAUDETTE cries more.)

CHUCK: Jimmie, just go home. Go home now.

ROBERT-EARL: No. He come to apologize. Let him apologize. I'll be the bigger man.

CHUCK: For real? You alright?

ROBERT-EARL: I'm alright. Yeah.

(CHUCK gets out of the way. ROBERT-EARL opens the door and then grabs JIMMIE and pulls him in)

ROBERT-EARL: I lied.

(CLAUDETTE screams. CHUCK and GERTIE run to ROBERT-EARL and pull him off JIMMIE.)

CHUCK: Robert-Earl, he ain't worth. He ain't worth it.

GERTIE: No. No. Stop it. Robert-Earl, stop it.

(ROBBIE is drawn out of her room by the ruckus in the living room. ROBERT-EARL tries to break free but CHUCK and GERTIE continue to hold ROBERT-EARL back.)

ROBERT-EARL: You kicked my daughter out of the house and into the goddamn street with all kinds of K-K-K and crackers roaming and preying, looking for niggers and you threw her out into the black night like a piece of motherfucking trash.

JIMMIE: She spit in my face. She hawked and spit in my face.

ROBERT-EARL: I don't give a damn what she did.

JIMMIE: She went like this.

(JIMMIE *hawks and spits right in* ROBERT-EARL's *face.*)

(*Jaws drop.*)

CHUCK: Beat his ass!

(ROBERT-EARL *breaks loose and charges* JIMMIE *and ploughs him into the dining room table.*)

GERTIE: Stop it. Stop it.

(JIMMIE *picks up a beer bottle from the dining room table and raises it in the air.*)

CLAUDETTE: Jimmie!

(JIMMIE *holds the bottle in the air as a weapon to keep* ROBERT-EARL *at bay.*)

JIMMIE: Claudette, we're going home.

CLAUDETTE: I don't wanna go with you.

JIMMIE: I said we're going home.

(JIMMIE *storms over to* CLAUDETTE *and grabs her by the arm with force.*)

ROBERT-EARL: Don't you grab my daughter.

(ROBERT-EARL *grabs* JIMMIE *and flings him to the ground. He pins* JIMMIE *down and begins to pummel him with punches.*)

ROBERT-EARL: I'll kill you.

GERTIE: Oh my God. Please don't.

(CHUCK and GERTIE *try to pull* ROBERT-EARL *off* JIMMIE *but they are no match for the adrenaline rush of* ROBERT-EARL's *anger.* ROBERT-EARL *kicks* JIMMIE *in the stomach.* JIMMIE *screams out in pain. He kicks* JIMMIE *in the stomach again.*)

ROBERT-EARL: I'll kill you. I'll kill you.

(ROBERT-EARL *kicks* JIMMIE *again. With each kick* ROBBIE *begins to back up into the corner by the shotgun.)*

CLAUDETTE: Daddy stop it.

(ROBBIE *bumps into the shotgun. The final kick sends her someplace else and she grabs the shotgun. She points it at* ROBERT-EARL. *Her breathing is shallow and harsh.)*

ROBBIE: Leave him alone.

(Everyone turns, finally noticing ROBBIE *with the shotgun.)*

ROBERT-EARL: You're gonna shoot me?

ROBBIE: I said get away from him.

(ROBERT-EARL *motions as if he's about to kick* JIMMIE *again.* ROBBIE *cocks the trigger. Her eyes are almost vacant.* ROBERT-EARL *stops)*

ROBBIE: What did I say?

(ROBERT-EARL *backs away from* JIMMIE. CLAUDETTE *runs to her husband's side.)*

GERTIE: Robbie, put the gun down.

(ROBBIE *still has the gun aimed at* ROBERT-EARL. GERTIE *slowly goes to* ROBBIE *and gets her to lower the gun. Then she takes the gun out daughter's hand. She gives the gun to* CHUCK. GERTIE *looks* ROBBIE *in the eyes and sees that her daughter isn't there.* GERTIE *slaps* ROBBIE *hard in the face to bring her back.)*

(The phone rings. CHUCK *answers it.)*

CHUCK: Hello.

(A loud shot is heard outside.)

CHUCK: What the hell?

ROBERT-EARL: That was a rifle.

(CHUCK *and* ROBERT-EARL *run outside.* ROBBIE *and* GERTIE *freeze.* CLAUDETTE *goes to the door.)*

CLAUDETTE: Folks are running to Medgar's house. Something happened at Medgar Evers' house.

(JIMMIE *pulls himself up and staggers out of the house.* CLAUDETTE *follows him.*)

(Chaos is heard outside.)

(ROBBIE *runs to the door. But* GERTIE *slams it shut and blocks it.*)

(Tense stand-off)

ROBBIE: Mama…mama…please…

GERTIE: No.

ROBBIE: Please. Let me go.

GERTIE: No.

ROBBIE: Mama.
Mama.
Let Me Go.

(GERTIE *grabs* ROBBIE. *And begins to force her further from the front door.* ROBBIE *tries to resist but* GERTIE's *grip is strong.*)

GERTIE: No. No. No. No. No.

(JIMMIE *comes back in. Startling* GERTIE)

JIMMIE: Medgar…Medgar…
He…
Almost made it to his front door.

(JIMMIE *grabs his stomach, covers his mouth and races to the bathroom.* ROBBIE *pulls away from* GERTIE *and runs out of the house.*)

GERTIE: Robbie!

(GERTIE *starts after* ROBBIE *but the phone rings. She stops in her tracks.*)

(GERTIE *stops and stares at the phone. Paralyzed as it rings. It rings. And rings. And rings.*)

(Finally GERTIE *charges for the phone and picks it up and raises it high ready to slam it to the floor—)*

(Abrupt black out)

END OF ACT ONE

ACT TWO

Scene One

(Four years earlier)

(1959)

(Lights up. The front door is wide open.)

(Poison Ivy by The Coasters plays on the kitchen radio.)

(After a beat, MYRLIE EVERS enters, dressed for business. She carries a briefcase. She stands cautiously near the front door, not wanting to go any farther without being welcomed. She looks around for some sign of life. She stands waiting for a good beat until...)

(GERTIE comes out of the kitchen, dressed for important company. She carries a tray of finger foods. She shakes her hips to the music on the radio. Then she sees MYRLIE and stops dancing.)

GERTIE: Oh. Mrs Evers. You're here.

(GERTIE runs back to the kitchen and turns off the radio. Then she comes back out.)

MYRLIE: Your door was standing wide open.

GERTIE: I let my daughter go to a friends'house. Look like she left the door wide open. Twelve year olds.

(GERTIE giggles. MYRLIE doesn't reciprocate.)

GERTIE: Please, have a seat. Make yourself comfortable.

(GERTIE and MYRLIE sit.)

GERTIE: Where is Mr Evers?

MYRLIE: My husband is running late. He'll be here soon.

GERTIE: Well don't feel bad. My husband is running late as well.

MYRLIE: It's for the best. Mrs Monroe, I wanted to have a moment to speak with you alone.

GERTIE: Yes, of course. Whatev—

MYRLIE: Are you the same Gertrude Monroe who wrote an opinion piece in the Jackson Advocate?

GERTIE: Yes ma'am. I am. You read it?

MYRLIE: Several times. I told my husband about it but he refused to read it.

GERTIE: Well, I hope there are no hard feelings. It wasn't meant against you or your husband, personally. I simply expressed my opinion as a Jackson-area Negro wife, mother and educator my disagreement with your activities. I just believe that many times your actions 'cause more trouble for Negroes. And I don't see the positive in any of it.
(Beat)
But that's just my opinion.

(Quiet for a beat. Then GERTIE gestures to the food. MYRLIE cuts her off before she can finish the sentence)

GERTIE: Would you like some—

MYRLIE: No thank you. I ate before I came.

GERTIE: *(Ice)* I see.

(ROBBIE comes into the house wearing a cute summer dress. She does not have a scar on her palm.)

ROBBIE: Mama I don't like this dress. I want to wear a different dress.

GERTIE: What's wrong with the dress?

ROBBIE: It's too dressy. Nobody else is dressed up. Sarah looked at me funny.

GERTIE: Well change your dress and hurry. And get back to the party.

ROBBIE: Yes ma'am.
(She sees MYRLIE*)*
Do we have company?
(Goes to MYRLIE*)*
Hello. I'm Roberta. So nice to meet you.

MYRLIE: Nice to meet you, too. I am—

ROBBIE: Miss Myrlie Evers. I saw you in the newspaper.

*(*ROBBIE *extends her hand.* ROBBIE *and* MYRLIE *shake.)*

ROBBIE: What's in your briefcase?

MYRLIE: Paperwork.

ROBBIE: What kind of paperwork?

GERTIE: Roberta stop being fresh.

ROBBIE: I'm not being fresh. It's just that I've never seen a Negro lady with a briefcase before. It makes you look so important. I want to look like you one day.

GERTIE: None of your business what is in her briefcase. Go change and hurry back to Sarah's house.

MYRLIE: It's okay. Its papers related to real estate matters. Your parents and I have business to settle.

ROBBIE: What kind of business?

GERTIE. Roberta, Go.

ROBBIE: Yes, ma'am.
(She goes to her room.)

GERTIE: Please keep my daughter out of this. She's only twelve.

MYRLIE: What did I do?

GERTIE: Real estate.

MYRLIE: Well it's the truth. Mrs Monroe, let's not pretend that we are here for any other reason—

GERTIE: She's too young to understand. That's not fair.

MYRLIE: What's not fair is—

(The door opens. It is CHUCK. *He carries a basket of tomatoes.)*

CHUCK: There is my Lovely.

GERTIE: Robert-Earl, you're home. Mrs Evers, this is my husband. Robert-Earl Monroe.

CHUCK: Mrs Myrlie Evers it is indeed a pleasure to meet you. And Mr Evers?

MYRLIE: He's running late.
You look familiar. Do you work on Farish Street?

CHUCK: No I coach high school football.

MYRLIE: That's what my husband said but seems that I know you from—

CHUCK: We're neighbors of course you know me.
(Laughs)
Mrs Evers, I brought you some tomatoes from my… sister's garden as a gift.

MYRLIE: Thank you.

*(*ROBBIE *comes out still in the same dress. comes out still in the same dress.)*

ROBBIE: Mama, where's my yellow—

CHUCK: There is my darling daughter. The apple of her father's eyes. Baby girl, how was school today?

*(*GERTIE *gives* CHUCK *a "Shut the hell up. That's not part of the plan" look.)*

ROBBIE: Fine.

(She stares at CHUCK.*)*

CHUCK: Roberta, your mother and I have company and would like privacy.

*(*ROBBIE *hurries to her room)*

CHUCK: Isn't she adorable? Oh how we've been blessed with two lovely daughters.

GERTIE: Roberta is the youngest. The oldest is Claudette. She is away at school. She's a sophomore at your alma mater, Alcorn. That's where you met Mr Evers.

MYRLIE: Yes. How did you know?

GERTIE: Well, we have important guests in our home. We did our research.

MYRLIE: I did my research too. Mrs Monroe, I understand that you are quite well connected and you are privileged to have some friends in very high places.

GERTIE: What do you mean?

MYRLIE: Did I say something wrong?

CHUCK: Well it looks like we've run out of small talk. Mrs Evers, I don't mean to be rude asking you this when your husband is not here but what are thoughts about our proposal? The offer?

MYRLIE: I will prefer to discuss this when my husband arrives.

CHUCK: Do you have the contract?

MYRLIE: Yes.

CHUCK: Can I see it?

MYRLIE: You don't have a copy?

CHUCK: Of course I do. But not on me. This was just meant to be a friendly gathering. An opportunity to discuss our differences and come to an understanding. But since you brought the contract—

MYRLIE: You can see the contract when my husband arrives.

CHUCK: Mrs Evers, there is no reason to be—

(ROBBIE storms into the living room.)

ROBBIE: I cannot remain silent any longer.
(Points to CHUCK)
He is—

CHUCK: Roberta, go to your room.

ROBBIE: No. That man is not my father.

MYRLIE: Excuse me?

ROBBIE: That's Mr Chuck. He lives down the street—

MYRLIE: What is going on?
(Beat)
Mrs Monroe. Please explain—

(GERTIE is at a loss.)

ROBBIE: Miss. Evers, does he even resemble me? No. That man is not my father. My father is a strong and handsome man.
(Points an accusing figure at CHUCK)
He is neither of those things.

MYRLIE: I thought you looked familiar. Smell familiar, too. You smell just like catfish from that café on Farish. Mrs Monroe?

(GERTIE, still at a loss. MYRLIE starts to leave, just as the door opens. It's ROBERT-EARL.)

ROBBIE: That's my daddy. Right there.

ROBERT-EARL: Pruitt? Gertie?
Why is everybody dressed up?

MYRLIE: Maybe you can get some answers. I'm done with it.

ROBERT-EARL: Myrlie Evers?

MYRLIE: Yes.

ROBERT-EARL: What is Myrlie Evers doing in my house?

MYRLIE: Leaving. That's what I'm doing.
(To ROBERT-EARL*)*
Will you please move away from the door so I can go home?

GERTIE: Robert-Earl, what happened to the football game?

ROBERT-EARL: The other team cancelled. Their quarterback's house was set on fire. His mama was burned real bad. She ain't gonna make it.
(To MYRLIE*)*
You're not here because of that are you? Look, we don't know nothing about that. We don't want no trouble.

MYRLIE: Typical.
(Charges ahead again)
Move please.

ROBBIE: Mr Chuck was pretending to be you, daddy. And mama was going right along with it. But I wasn't having it.

MYRLIE: Will someone please tell him to move?

(ROBERT-EARL *gestures for* ROBBIE *to go to her room. She does:)*

ROBERT-EARL: Gertie, you better talk—

(ROBERT-EARL *goes to* GERTIE. MYRLIE *reaches for the door knob. There is a knock at the door which startles* MYRLIE.

Then she looks out the window in the door. It is MEDGAR.
She opens the door.)

MEDGAR: I'm so sorry I'm late.

MYRLIE: Medgar, we're going home.

GERTIE: Please don't leave. We can explain.

MEDGAR: Excuse me?	ROBERT-EARL: Somebody need to explain something.
MYRLIE: Medgar, these people are playing—	CHUCK: Look now, we got business to handle. Ain't nobody going nowhere.
MEDGAR: Excuse me?	ROBERT-EARL: What business?
MYRLIE: Medgar, I said we're going—	CHUCK: The offer.

MYRLIE: And we're not accepting your offer. You
people should be ashamed of yourselves. You are
setting the Negro race back a hundred years. Medgar,
we're leaving.

MEDGAR: *(Gives* MYRLIE *a look)* What was that?

MYRLIE: *(Pissed)* Mr Evers—
Please take me home now!

MEDGAR: Mrs Evers, I need you to take a moment and
calm down—

(MYRLIE *storms out of the house.)*

MEDGAR: *(Calling out after his wife)* Mrs Evers! Mrs
Evers! Mrs Evers!

CHUCK: They call each other Mr and Mrs Evers. What
the hell kind of shit?

MEDGAR: My wife and I work together. She is my secretary and when we handle official business we refer to each other in professional terms.

GERTIE: Official business? This is just a nice neighborly gathering.

MEDGAR: A neighborly gathering to convince us to move out of the neighborhood. If we bother you so much then you should leave the neighborhood. You'll never have to worry about my family again.

CHUCK: It's not your family that's the problem. It's you.

MEDGAR: Now look here. I am not the enemy. I am a Negro trying to survive in the treacherous state of Mississippi same as you. Born and raised and determined to die here. No one is going to run me out of this state or off this street.

CHUCK: Well maybe some of us don't think things are that bad off. I remember a time when things were much worse.

(ROBBIE *pokes her head out and listens from the hallway.*)

MEDGAR: But don't you want something better for your children?
(Notices ROBBIE*)*
For that little girl standing right there. A better Mississippi than the one you inherited? You folks from Mississippi?

ROBERT-EARL: *(Nods to* CHUCK*)* We both from Vicksburg.

MEDGAR: My wife's from Vicksburg. Mrs Monroe?

GERTIE: ...Money.

MEDGAR: Money, Mississippi?

ROBERT-EARL: That's what she said.

MEDGAR: Did you know Emmett Ti—

(GERTIE *cuts* MEDGAR *off.* ROBBIE *tenses then quickly goes to her room.*)

GERTIE: We don't say his name in this house.

(Beat)

It used to give Roberta nightmares. Still does sometimes.

MEDGAR: I'm sorry. Did Roberta know—

GERTIE: No. She saw his picture in the Jet magazine. I need to see about my child.

(She leaves the room to see about ROBBIE.*)*

ROBERT-EARL: You upset my daughter. And my wife.

MEDGAR: I'm sorry. I didn't know.

ROBERT-EARL: You did too know. When she said Money you should have left it alone.

CHUCK: He agitating. That's all he do. He agitates. He a troublemaker.

(To MEDGAR*)*

Why don't you just take the offer and leave us alone.

ROBERT-EARL: What offer?

MEDGAR: We're not selling.

CHUCK: You got a nice offer. I'd take it.

MEDGAR: I don't want the money.

ROBERT-EARL: Chuck, what the hell y'all talking about?

MEDGAR: What do you mean what the hell we're talking about? Your name is on the contract.

ROBERT-EARL: What contract?

MEDGAR: I don't have time for this.

*(*MEDGAR *leaves. Slamming the door.* GERTIE *comes out.)*

GERTIE: Did he slam the door? Did he slam the door?

ROBERT-EARL: Gertie, you know anything about a contract?

(GERTIE *looks at* CHUCK.)

ROBERT-EARL: What you looking at Chuck for? Look at me. Answer the question.

GERTIE: Robert-Earl, I can explain.

ROBERT-EARL: Well, I'm waiting.

CHUCK: Monroe, don't be sore at Gertie. It was all my idea.
(Beat)
We came into some money and we were trying to buy the Evers out of their house.

ROBERT-EARL: How much money?

CHUCK: Ten thousand dollars.

ROBERT-EARL: Ten thousand dollars? How do you just happen to come into ten thousand dollars?

CHUCK: Some of my business associates donated the money.

ROBERT-EARL: Who donates ten thousand dollars to Negroes? And what that gotta do with Gertie?

GERTIE: We're the family that made the offer to buy the house. Your name is on the contract—I forged your signature—
Robert-Earl, that much money, I thought they'd sign the papers easy and you'd never know—

ROBERT-EARL: How I'm not gonna know when I got two houses in my name?

GERTIE: The house wouldn't belong to us. We would hand it over to Chuck's business associates. Transfer the papers and that would be the end of it.

ROBERT-EARL: Pruitt, what kind of scheme you got my wife wrapped up in?

CHUCK: I didn't drag Gertie into anything. I'm trying to help.

(Beat)

Gertie, tell your husband what's going on.

(GERTIE *is silent.*)

CHUCK: He has a right to know. It's only decent—

ROBERT-EARL: Oh. Now I got a right to know.

CHUCK: Let her talk.

(GERTIE *takes a moment to speak.*)

GERTIE: We need the money…for Claudette's tuition.

ROBERT-EARL: Claudette is on full scholarship. We don't need no damn tuition money.

GERTIE: Yes we do.

(Her face breaks. She runs to her bedroom.)

ROBERT-EARL: Gertie! Gertie!

(He runs after her. We hear banging on the bedroom door)

Gertie. Open this door. Gertie. Gertie.

(The banging grows louder and more threatening. ROBBIE *comes into the living room. Drawn out of her room by the banging)*

ROBERT-EARL: Gertie, you're scaring me. Open this door. What's wrong with Claudette? Don't make me break down this door. Open this damn door.

CHUCK: Dammit Robert-Earl!

(CHUCK *runs back to* ROBERT-EARL. *More banging)*

CHUCK: *(O S)* Robert-Earl, Robert-Earl! Stop. Stop. Shit.

(The sound intensifies as if ROBERT-EARL *is banging his body against the door)*

CHURCK: MONROE!

(There is a knock at the door. ROBBIE *is scared. She doesn't knowvwhat to do. She doesn't answer the door. Another knock at the door.)*

ROBERT-EARL: *(O S)* Get your hands off me, Chuck. Get your hands off me.

*(*ROBBIE *runs closer to the front door to get away from the hallway. The front door opens. It's* MEDGAR. *He steps inside.)*

MEDGAR: Is everything okay?

(A loud crashing sound. ROBERT-EARL *broke down the door.* GERTIE *screams.* ROBBIE *cries out and runs to* MEDGAR *for protection.* MEDGAR *holds* ROBBIE *in him arms. She cries.)*

MEDGAR: It's okay. It's okay.

*(*ROBERT-EARL *comes into the living room, nursing his shoulder.)*

ROBERT-EARL: Shit—
Shit—
Shit—
Gertie. I didn't mean to break down the door. Gertie, come out please. Talk to me 'bout Claudette, damn.
(Looks at MEDGAR*)*
What are you doing here?

MEDGAR: My wife left the briefcase.

*(*CHUCK *comes into the living room. Soon followed by* GERTIE.*)*

ROBERT-EARL: Then take the briefcase and go.

MEDGAR: *(Takes out his handkerchief and wipes* ROBBIE'*s eyes)* Are you going to be okay?

*(*ROBBIE *nods her head "yes")*

MEDGAR: You sure? Smile. I'm not leaving till I see you smile a little bit. Do you feel like smiling?

*(*ROBBIE *gives a weak smile.)*

MEDGAR: Ahhhhh, you can do better than that.

(ROBBIE *gives a bigger smile.* MEDGAR *smiles in return.*)

MEDGAR: There ya go. You okay?

(ROBBIE *nods "yes".* MEDGAR *takes the briefcase*)

MEDGAR: You all take care now.

ROBBIE: Mr Evers, Thursday is my thirteenth birthday. And my mom always makes me a special dinner the night before my birthday. Would you like to come Wednesday night.

MEDGAR: I'll check my schedule.
(He leaves.)

ROBERT-EARL: Roberta!

CHUCK: This might be a blessing in disguise. If he comes to the birthday dinner—

ROBERT-EARL: Pruitt, go home. I need to talk to Gertie alone.

CHUCK: Roberta, you wanna come with me? Play with Lucy. She likes it when you rub her tummy.

ROBBIE: Yes sir.

GERTIE: What about the party at Sarah's house?

ROBBIE: I don't feel like going back.
(Beat)
I found my yellow dress. It doesn't fit me anymore.

(CHUCK *and* ROBBIE *leave.*)

ROBERT-EARL: Well?

GERTIE: Robert-Earl, we're in very bad trouble. Very bad. Claudette's scholarship has been taken away—

ROBERT-EARL: Why?

GERTIE: I got myself into a situation and as punishment, Claudette lost her scholarship and the school is going to send her home—

ROBERT-EARL: Who is going to send her home?

GERTIE: The school. The school. Who do you think? And it's all my fault. I did something wrong and it's all my fault.

ROBERT-EARL: What did you do?

GERTIE: I don't know. I don't know what I did. But I'm in trouble. And now Claudette is being punished and the only way we can keep her in school is to get the Evers to sell their house.

ROBERT-EARL: Gertie, this isn't making sense.

GERTIE: It makes perfect sense. If they don't sell their house, Claudette gets kicked out of college.

ROBERT-EARL: Why did the school take away her scholarship?

GERTIE: Because of something I did.

ROBERT-EARL: What did you do?

GERTIE: I told you I don't know.

ROBERT-EARL: Have you talked to Claudette?

GERTIE: I tried to call her twice. Both times I got the dorm mother. And then yesterday I called and the dean said there's nothing he could do but pay her way home on Greyhound.

ROBERT-EARL: I don't understand what's happening.

GERTIE: They got my name on a list. They got all of us on a list. Your name. My name. The girls' names. The girls' schools. Our jobs. Our address. The license plate of our car. They got all our information.
(Beat)
It's a very bad list, Robert-Earl. And it's all my fault.

(Lights out.)

(End of scene)

Scene Two

(Two evenings later, after dinner.)

(MEDGAR, MYRLIE and ROBBIE sit in the living room.)

ROBBIE: Have you ever met Lena Horne?

MEDGAR: Yes.

ROBBIE: Have you ever met Nat King Cole?

MEDGAR: No.

ROBBIE: Have you ever met Ella Fitzgerald?

MEDGAR: No.

ROBBIE: Have you ever met Martin Luther King?

(MYRLIE giggles.)

MEDGAR: You said that one already. Yes.

ROBBIE: Have you ever met President Eisenhower?

MEDGAR: No.

(ROBBIE is at a loss. Struggling for a new name)

MYRLIE: I think she's running out of people.

ROBBIE: Have you ever met…have you ever met…have you ever met…Desi Arnez.

MYRLIE: Desi Arnez? From *I Love Lucy*?

(Everyone laughs.)

MEDGAR: No.

(There is a knock at the door.)

GERTIE: *(O S—from the kitchen)* I'll get it.

(GERTIE comes out. She opens the door. It is CHUCK. He brings a homemade cake.)

CHUCK: Where is the almost birthday girl?

ROBBIE: Here I am!

(Sees the cake)

Did you make my favorite?

CHUCK: Yes ma'am.

(He takes the top off the container.)

CHUCK & ROBBIE: German Chocolate.

GERTIE: Chuck, you missed the dinner.

CHUCK: Some bullshit down at the café kept me longer than I wanted. Where's Robert-Earl?

GERTIE: He went to pick-up Roberta's birthday present from the secret hiding place.

CHUCK: Miss Lottie?

GERTIE: It's supposed to be a secret. Now next year we're going to have to change the hiding place.

CHUCK: *(To* MEDGAR *and* MYRLIE*)* Hello folks. How you?

MEDGAR: Fine and you?

CHUCK: Can't complain.

MYRLIE: Mr Evers, I believe we should be leaving now.

CHUCK: Awwwwwwwww hell. Y'all still on that Mr and Mrs nonsense? This ain't official business. This is a child's birthday. Let your hair down. Live a little. Shit.

MEDGAR: Well actually we are here on official business. We are here to present Roberta with this pin—

*(*MYRLIE *pulls a pin out of her purse.)*

MEDGAR: —declaring her as an Honorary Junior Executive Member of the National Association for the Advancement of Colored People.

*(*MYRLIE *pins* ROBBIE*.)*

ROBBIE: I've never been an Honorary Member of anything. This is so exciting. Do I get my name listed on something?

GERTIE: NO!

(Beat)

Her name will not be listed. Will it?

MYRLIE: It'll be on the rolls at the national office in New York City.

(Beat. A little sharp)

No one in Mississippi will ever see the list. If that is what you're worried about.

(GERTIE's come-back is interrupted by the door opening. ROBERT-EARL comes in with a brand new bicycle.)

ROBERT-EARL: *(Singing)*
Happy Birthday to you.

ROBERT-EARL, GERTIE, MEDGAR, MYRLIE, & CHUCK:
Happy Birthday to you.
Happy Birthday dear Roberta.
Happy Birthday to you.

CHUCK: Let's cut the cake.

(GERTIE goes to get plates and forks.)

GERTIE: Oh…oh…Robert-Earl. Get the camera so we can take a picture of Roberta with her new bicycle.

ROBBIE: Is that the bike we saw downtown in the store window at Woolworth's?

GERTIE: Yes it is.

ROBBIE: Yay!

(She jumps up and down with excitement. She runs to the bike and begins to admire it.)

MEDGAR: Woolworth's?

GERTIE: Yes sir. Woolworth. Saw it in the window. Roberta had a fit.

MEDGAR: They won't let Negroes eat at the lunch counters at Woolworth's. Folks talking about protesting all over the South. We shouldn't support them anymore.

CHUCK: I don't see the problem, myself. You can't eat at the white folks lunch counter, come on over to my café. It all works out.

MEDGAR: Well that's not the point.

CHUCK: It is the point. Negroes crying because they can't eat at the white folks' lunch counters. When they know there is plenty good food just waiting for them on Farish Street. Anything you can find downtown at the white stores you can find on Farish just as nice.

MEDGAR: I'm not contesting that but if our money is good enough to shop in their stores then it's good enough to purchase a meal at their lunch counters.

ROBERT-EARL: Are you saying that we should return the bicycle?

MYRLIE: No. That's not what he's saying.
(Beat)
After all, you can't take away her birthday present.

MEDGAR: Actually Mrs Evers, I think they should return the bicycle.

GERTIE: I bought that bicycle and I'm not returning it. And furthermore, I do the shopping for this family. And no outside influence is going to tell me where I can and cannot shop.

MYRLIE: The bicycle stays.
(Smiles. A little flirtatious. She touches her husband's shoulder)
Mr Evers, please. For me.

*(*MEDGAR *gives* MYRLIE *a LOOK. She quickly removes her hand.)*

MEDGAR: She can keep the bike, I suppose. But you shouldn't shop there anymore.

CHUCK: Hear, hear! And take all your money on over to Farish Street.

MEDGAR: But the point is. Change is coming to Mississippi.

(MYRLIE *ain't feeling him no more. She has a "Give it a rest" look on her face,*)

MEDGAR: And we all have to do our part in the fight for equality.
Don't you want change?

(MEDGAR *gets blank stares.*)

ROBERT-EARL: Roberta, Miss Lottie said she'll be sitting on the front porch for a good spell. Go outside and ride your bike.

ROBBIE: Yes sir.

GERTIE: Baby…
(*She goes to* ROBBIE *and takes the pin off.*)
Did you do anything to earn this?

ROBBIE: No ma'am.

GERTIE: That's right. You have to earn an honor. Now give it back to the Evers.

(ROBBIE *hands the pin back to* MEDGAR.)

ROBBIE: Thank you. But I can't keep this. Mama says I have to earn it.

MEDGAR: Maybe one day you will.

(MEDGAR *smiles.* ROBBIE *takes her bike and goes outside.* MEDGAR'*s smile disappears.*)

MEDGAR: That pin was a birthday present. Just like that bicycle was a birthday present.

MYRLIE: Thank you for inviting us. We should leave now.

MEDGAR: Miss Evers, no. This is not finished yet. Because first of all, they did not invite us. Their daughter did. And second, they have no right to refuse a gift that wasn't given to them.

GERTIE: She's our daughter and we have a say in what organizations she joins. You have to get our permission first. Especially for an organization we do not approve of.

MYRLIE: We understand.

(Beat)

Good evening.

(MYRLIE goes to the door. MEDGAR does not move.)

MYRLIE: Med—Mr Evers?

MEDGAR: Mrs Evers, we're not leaving. We have some unsettled business before we go. We've considered your offer and we have decided that we're not interested in selling our home.

CHUCK: Fifteen thousand dollars say you change your mind. That's twice what the house is worth.

MEDGAR: No amount of money is going to change our mind.

MYRLIE: Mr Evers, that's a lot of money.

MEDGAR: Money isn't everything, *Mrs Evers*.

MYRLIE: I'm not saying that it is. *Mr Evers*. But that's still a lot of money and we should have a discussion— in private about this first. Weigh all options.

MEDGAR: There's nothing to discuss. We're not for sale and neither is our home. Now we can leave.

(MEDGAR goes to the door. MYRLIE doesn't move.)

MEDGAR: Mrs Evers?

MYRLIE: I'll see you at the house.

MEDGAR: What's wrong?

MYRLIE: I need to go to the ladies room, first

MEDGAR: Then I'll wait.

MYRLIE: Don't.
(She hurries off to the bathroom. She slams the door.)

CHUCK: She's maaaaaaaaaaaaaaad at you.

(MEDGAR storms out of the house)

CHUCK: We got Myrlie in our corner—

GERTIE: She didn't say for sure.

CHUCK: Oh she's in our corner. I can tell. She wants that money. We got to work on her. Get her to press Medgar. Press him till he can't say no.

ROBERT-EARL: I'll get the contracts.

GERTIE: It's in the china cabinet.

(ROBERT-EARL goes to the china cabinet. He searches through the drawers.)

ROBERT-EARL: How much time do we have?

GERTIE: Time for what?

ROBERT-EARL: Claudette's school.

GERTIE: God I don't want to think about it.

ROBERT-EARL: How much?

GERTIE: They're gonna put her on a bus home tomorrow morning. We have to get the papers signed tonight.

ROBERT-EARL: I don't see contracts. Where are they?

GERTIE: They're folded in the middle of the family Bible.

(ROBERT-EARL finds the Bible and the contracts.)

ROBERT-EARL: Pruitt, you for real about the fifteen thousand dollars?

CHUCK: Hell yeah I'm for real.

(MYRLIE *comes out just in time to be treated to a sampling of Chuck's poetic eloquence*)

CHUCK: Is pig pussy pork?

MYRLIE: I should be going now.

CHUCK: Miss Evers, I did not see you standing there. I apologize for my language. Please don't run off on account of me.

MYRLIE: No. I need to go home and talk to Mr Evers. (*She moves to the front door.*)

CHUCK: Mrs Evers, fifteen thousand dollars is nothing to sniff at. I believe you understand that. But your husband on the other hand.

GERTIE: Help us. To help you.

MYRLIE: How do I do that?

GERTIE: Please have a seat.

CHUCK: And please. Have some cake. You look like you should eat something.

MYRLIE: We've already eaten.

CHUCK: You need something sweet. You look peekiddy. Like you're getting sickly.

ROBERT-EARL: Gertie, get her some cake and something to drink.

(GERTIE *slices the cake and takes a piece to* MYRLIE.)

ROBERT-EARL: Would you like anything to drink?

GERTIE: Water? Coffee? Tea?

MYRLIE: I'm fine. Really. I need to go home.

GERTIE: You should sit a spell. You look upset and worried—

MYRLIE: Of course I'm—
This has turned out to be one of the most unpleasant evenings—

ROBERT-EARL: Now that's not fair. It's not our fault. Your husband is the one that caused confusion. Arguing with us over a bicycle and such. We just meant to have a friendly birthday celebration for my daughter.

GERTIE: I really wish you'd take a bite of the cake. It would make me feel better. And it would make you feel better too.

MYRLIE: It's your daughter's birthday cake. She should have the first bite.
(She puts the cake down.)
I'm not hungry.

GERTIE: *(To the men)* Can we have time alone?

ROBERT-EARL: Why?

CHUCK: Monroe, let's leave the women alone for a moment. Give them some time to talk lady talk. Let's go out back. Have a smoke.

(ROBERT-EARL and CHUCK leave the room.)

GERTIE: Mrs Evers, you and I both know that while the husband is the head, it's the wife that truly knows what is best for her family. For her children. And it is her responsibility to act on that knowledge in any and all ways necessary to ensure the wellbeing of her home. Sometimes men are stubborn and can't see the forest for the trees. If we don't steer them in the right direction, then whatever trouble befalls the family is our fault.

MYRLIE: What trouble?

GERTIE: I'm just going to come out and say it. I worry about your family. I do. I really do. There are sick people in Mississippi who do horrible things to Negroes. Especially Negroes they don't like.

MYRLIE: You really think you're telling me something I don't know? Medgar knows the danger and he's not afraid. Threats to his life—

GERTIE: I'm not talking about your husband. I'm talking about your babies. And I'm not making this up. I'm not assuming. I'm telling you what I know. What I've heard.

(Beat)

I'm trying to help you. No one talks to you on Guyenes Street. If I don't tell you, who will?

MYRLIE: It's true.

GERTIE: What?

MYRLIE: What I've heard about you is all true. It's not heresay.

GERTIE: I don't know what you're talking about.

MYRLIE: Those white folks you're working for. They're not your friends.

GERTIE: I don't work for white folks.

MYRLIE: Yes you do. The Mississippi Sovereignty Commission. They're not your friend.

GERTIE: I don't know what that even is.

MYRLIE: You will. Soon. I promise you. You've opened that door. And once it's opened. You can't close it back. *(She stands.)*

Goodnight. Mrs Monroe.

(She goes to the door to leave.)

GERTIE: Your children's lives are in danger. There is a pamphlet circulating with your children's faces on it.

And they're names and nicknames and what kind of ice-cream they like. What sports your son likes.

MYRLIE: I teach my children not to trust white people unless I give them the okay. So I can assure you that my children will not be fooled—

GERTIE: Mrs Evers—

MYRLIE: And I never let my children out of my sight except for school.

GERTIE: Really? Where are they now?

MYRLIE: At home with their father.

GERTIE: Where were they before your husband got home?

MYRLIE: They were being looked after by a student from Tougaloo.

GERTIE: How well do you know the student?

MYRLIE: You are a horrible, horrible woman.

GERTIE: I am trying to be a friend.

MYRLIE: A friend? We've lived on this street two years. And until a week ago we had never spoken.

GERTIE: I was afraid.

MYRLIE: To have us in your home?

GERTIE: Yes.

MYRLIE: Then why aren't you afraid now?

GERTIE: I am afraid. But we have an opportunity to make things better for all the families on this street. For your family especially. Take the money.

MYRLIE: And where do we go?

GERTIE: You can find a place near Tougaloo. You'd fit in there and it would be safer for your family—

MYRLIE: How would it be safer?

GERTIE: More like-minded people I suppose. Folks who would come to your aid if something happened.

MYRLIE: You saying you wouldn'tcome to our aid?

GERTIE: Fear is a powerful thing, Mrs Evers. I really don't know what I would do. And I don't ever want anything to happen to make me have to confront that.

(The door opens. ROBBIE comes in with her bicycle.)

GERTIE: Go around the back with your bike. Don't roll it through the house.

ROBBIE: Miss Lottie made me come in the house. Some white men riding through. Miss Lottie said look like they up to no good.

GERTIE: Then put your bike out back and go in your room.

ROBBIE: But I want some German Chocolate.

GERTIE: After company leaves.

ROBBIE: But company is for me.

GERTIE: What did I say?

(ROBBIE takes her bicycle out back.)

MYRLIE: I'm going home.

GERTIE: Not with those men outside.

MYRLIE: I'll take my chances.
(She gets up to leave.)

GERTIE: I'd prefer they not see you leave our house.

(MYRLIE sits.)

GERTIE: Thank you.

(ROBBIE comes in the room with ROBERT-EARL and CHUCK.)

ROBERT-EARL: Roberta, go to your room, get still.

ROBBIE: I know. I know.

CHUCK: Goddamit. These crackers at it again.

(ROBERT-EARL and CHUCK go out the front door. The phone rings. GERTIE answers.)

GERTIE: Hello.

(Beat)

One moment, please.

(To MYRLIE)

It's for you.

MYRLIE: *(Takes the phone)*

Hello—

I'll be home in a little bit—

A little bit—

Are the kids okay—

I didn't say they can leave the house with her—

What were you thinking—

I'm coming home—

(She hangs up the phone.)

GERTIE: Please. Just wait till it's safe.

(She moves in front of the door.)

MYRLIE: This is Mississippi. Negroes are never safe. Get used to it.

(The door opens bumping GERTIE out the way. ROBERT-EARL and CHUCK rush in. MYRLIE rushes out.)

ROBERT-EARL: Dammit. You let her leave. Get her back.

CHUCK: Is she going to get Medgar to sign the contract?

GERTIE: No. I don't know yet.

ROBERT-EARL: Is she close?

GERTIE: I DON'T KNOW!

ROBERT-EARL: Don't yell at me. You got us into this.

(There is a knocking at the door. Everyone is startled. The door opens. MYRLIE *rushes in—in a panic.* CHUCK *stays by the window and looks out.)*

MYRLIE: Some white man sitting outside our house. Sitting on the hood of our car. Sitting on the hood like it belongs to him. I need to call Medgar.
(She picks up the phone.)
Operator. Please give me 2332 Guynes.
(Beat)
Pick up.
Pick up.
Why isn't he picking up?
Pick up, Medgar.

CHUCK: Shit. Get off the phone. Get off the phone. They're outside the house.

GERTIE: What?

CHUCK: There's a white man parked outside the house. Get off the phone. Everybody be quiet. Everybody be still.

*(*MYRLIE *hangs up the phone.* CHUCK *remains by the window.)*

MYRLIE: I think I recognize the man. Sitting on the hood of our car. I've seen him before.

GERTIE: At some point you're going to have to take matters into your own hands. You can't keep living like this. We can't keep living like this.
(She grabs the contracts and a pen. She means business.)

MYRLIE: He's not going to sign those.

GERTIE: Where are your children?

MYRLIE: They're with the babysitter.

GERTIE: Why did your husband let her take them?

MYRLIE: I don't know.

ROBERT-EARL: Maybe he knew something was about to happen. Maybe he was trying to get them out of the house. He sho' didn't warn nobody.

GERTIE: But where are they now? Are they safe? You don't know. Do you?

CHUCK: Goddamn. Another car just pulled up.
He's coming to the door.

(ROBERT-EARL goes to his bedroom. MYRLIE runs into a far corner. GERTIE stays put. Frozen. There is a knock at the door. ROBERT-EARL comes back out with the shotgun. He goes to the front door and gestures for CHUCK to go man the kitchen door. CHUCK goes. More knocking. Then the knocking turns to banging. ROBBIE comes out her room. Then CHUCK pokes his head out of the kitchen. He holds a butcher knife. More banging. ROBBIE sees the knife and runs back to her room.)

ROBERT-EARL: Who is it?
(No response)
Who is it?

GERTIE: *(To MYRLIE)* Is this how you want to keep living your life?

ROBERT-EARL: Who is it?
(No response)
They are ladies in this house and a little girl. And you are scaring them.
I have a shotgun.
Who is it?
I have a gun and I will use it if you make me.
(Still no response)
Chuck, go stand by the back door.

(CHUCK's eyes are fixed on the front door)

ROBERT-EARL: Somebody goin' round back. Move. Shit.

(CHUCK goes back into the kitchen.)

GERTIE: Do what's best for your children. If he won't sign the papers. You do it for him.

ROBERT-EARL: Gertie, don't make no noise. Just be quiet.

(GERTIE and MYRLIE speak in hushed tones.)

MYRLIE: I can't do that.

GERTIE: You have to do something. For your children. Sign the papers and make him move.

MYRLIE: How do I do that? How?

GERTIE: *(Getting increasingly louder)* Tell him you will leave him. Tell him that you will take the children and leave him, if he doesn't agree to move. You will go back home to your people and he will never see his babies again. You have the power to do that. And you have the right.

MYRLIE: I don't have the right to do that.

ROBERT-EARL: I said shut-up.

(There is a loud, and violent banging at the backdoor. Like someone trying to kick the door in. CHUCK comes running into the living room. Holding the knife in the air.)

CHUCK: He coming round front. Motherfucker comin' to the front.

(There is a kick at the front door.)

ROBERT-EARL: I'll blow your ass away with my shotgun. I swear to God.

(Then without any more thought, MYRLIE quickly signs the contract. GERTIE gives her the second contract.)

GERTIE: This one too.

(MYRLIE starts to sign.)

(A car speeds off.)

(CHUCK looks out the window.)

CHUCK: Damn!

GERTIE: You're doing the right thing. For your babies.

(MYRLIE *starts to sign again.*)

(*There is a knock at the door.*)

MEDGAR: *(O S)* It's Mr Evers. I'm here to see Mrs Evers.

GERTIE: Sign the paper!

MEDGAR: *(O S)* Mrs Evers.

(MYRLIE *quickly begins to scratch through her signature on the first contract. Then she rips the contracts up. Tears in her eyes)+*

(ROBERT-EARL *puts the gun down. He nods for* CHUCK *to put the knife away.* CHUCK *stares* ROBERT-EARL *down. Tense for a moment.*)

MEDGAR: *(O S)* Open this door.

(CHUCK *storms off to the kitchen. Then he returns without the knife.* ROBERT-EARL *opens the door.* MEDGAR *comes in.*)

MEDGAR: Mrs Evers, it is time to go. Why are you crying?
Why is she crying?
Why is my—
Why is Mrs Evers crying?

(MYRLIE *gives* MEDGAR *a cutting look.*)

MYRLIE: Mrs Evers? Mrs Evers? I am your wife, Medgar. You see me standing here with tears in my eyes and you can't—
Some things are more important than your policies and procedures and protocol and the goddamn N-A-A-C-P.

(MYRLIE'*s face breaks. She tries to plough through* MEDGAR *to leave. He stops her. Tries to calm her. She pulls away from him.*)

MEDGAR: Everything will be fine. Please just let me take you home—
Mrs—

(MYRLIE stops.)

MYRLIE: I signed the papers. I forged your signature on that contract to sell the house. Then I tore up the papers. I couldn't go through with it. Don't make me regret tearing up the papers. I don't want to regret that. Don't make me.
(She breaks more. Inconsolable. She starts off to the bathroom. Her crying is so deep and harsh that she begins to crumble to the floor.)

GERTIE: Oh my God.

(ROBBIE comes into the living room and MYRLIE stumbles into ROBBIE on her way to the bathroom. ROBBIE catches hold to MYRLIE. MYRLIE struggles for air. MYRLIE clings to ROBBIE and doesn't let go. MEDGAR goes to MYRLIE. He walks her over to the living room chair and sits her down. ROBBIE stays attached.)

MEDGAR: It's okay. It's gonna be okay

(MYRLIE takes ROBBIE's hand and squeezes it tight. ROBBIE winces.)

MEDGAR: Breathe. Breathe. Mrs Evers. Mrs Evers. Mrs Evers.

(MYRLIE only makes it worse. She lets go of ROBBIE's hand.)

MEDGAR: Mrs Evers
(Finally he gets it.)
Myrlie. Myrlie. Myrlie.
(He picks her up from the chair and holds her close)
Myrlie.

(MYRLIE throws her arms around MEDGAR in a fierce embrace.)

MEDGAR: Let's go home.

(MEDGAR *takes his wife.* CHUCK *blocks the door.* MEDGAR *gives him a look that says "Don't try me."* CHUCK *moves.* MEDGAR *and*MYRLIE *leave.*)

CHUCK: Goddamn!

(*Quiet. Defeat. Stillness. Reckoning*)

ROBERT-EARL: What now?

(CHUCK *goes to the phone.*)

CHUCK: Operator give me 4023 West.
(*To* ROBBIE*)*
This is grown folks business.

(ROBBIE *goes to her room.*)

CHUCK: Them boys you sent didn't do their job right. They were supposed to stay outside till we gave the sign.
(*Beat*)
They drove off. They were supposed to stay outside banging on the damn door.
(*Beat*)
Gun? Yeah he had a gun.
(*To* ROBERT-EARL*)*
What you get the gun for?

ROBERT-EARL: I was trying to make it look good. Hell, you had a knife.

(ROBBIE *appears in the hallway entrance. She hides and listens. No one sees her.*)

CHUCK: I didn't announce I had a damn knife. Did I? The knife was to scare Myrlie. Shit.
(*Beat*)
Gertie, he wants to talk to you.

(GERTIE *takes the phone.*)

GERTIE: Hello—
No. She signed one of the contracts but then she tore it
up—
No we can't salvage it. But give us another chance.
Please. Please.
(Beat)
Hello. Hello. Hello—
He hung up.

ROBERT-EARL: Gertie, who are these people?

GERTIE: I don't know…they just white people…
(Beat)
One of the teachers at my school
One of the teachers at my school said she liked the
article I wrote about my—
Dislike— Of the Evers.
The article I wrote in the paper.
Said she agreed with me one-hundred percent.
Asked me if I would like to go to a meeting with her.
I went.
There was some white ladies at the meeting.
Really sweet—kind.
The kindest white folks I'd ever met.
Said we had something important in common.
We were all concerned citizens of Jackson.
Mothers who wanted what was best for our children.
And our children's children.
That we were all on the side of right.
They invited me to more a few more—meetings.
Always real nice.
Real good white people.
Then they started asking me to do—favors.
Go to meetings at church and get information.
At first I didn't want to
then I thought to myself

I spent seventeen years of my life fighting every day to
get out of Money, Mississippi.
And I swore when I left I'd never go back.
And I be damned if my girls ever experience the kind
of hell I lived through.
I owed it to my girls.
So I went to the church meetings—
and got the information they wanted.
I gave them the names.
(Beat)
I did.
I did that.
Several times.
But after a while, I didn't like myself much anymore.
I said I wanted to stop.
They weren't so nice anymore.
Said I can't stop.
I've opened a door. And I can't close it back.
(Beat)
I need to be alone.

*(GERTIE turns to go to the bedroom. She sees ROBBIE. Now
everyone notices her.)*

ROBERT-EARL: We told you to go to your room.

*(The phone rings. Startling everyone. ROBERT-EARL
answers.)*

ROBERT-EARL: Hello—
Claudette—
Baby—
Baby calm down—
Calm down—
Gertie, she wants to talk to you.

(GERTIE doesn't move.)

ROBERT-EARL: Take the phone, Gertie.

(GERTIE *takes and holds the phone. But she doesn't place it to her ear. She stares into* ROBBIE'*s confused eyes. Then she drops the phone and runs out of the room.*)

ROBERT-EARL: GERTIE!
(He picks up the phone and speaks)
Claudette? Claudette?
(She has hung up the phone.)
GODDAMN!
Gertie! Gertie!

(ROBERT-EARL *runs out of the room. A door slam.*)

CHUCK: How much did you hear?

(ROBBIE *doesn't answer. She shrugs her shoulders.* CHUCK *gives up and goes to the front door.*)

CHUCK: This a crying shame. That damn close.

(ROBBIE *is alone. After a beat, she goes to the dining table where the German Chocolate cake is. She stares at the cake for a moment.*)

ROBBIE: *(Singing, quietly)*
Happy Birthday to me.
Happy Birthday…
(Then she picks up the knife. She cuts a slice of cake)
Happy Birthday. Happy Birthday.

(Then she cuts another slice. She begins to jab the knife into the cake. Slow and deliberate at first and then picks up speed. Jabbing and jabbing.)

(In her speed and recklessness—her hand slips—slicing her palm wide open. She screams.)

(She takes a few steps then falls to the floor in pain.)

(ROBERT-EARL *comes out. Quickly followed by* GERTIE.)

ROBERT-EARL: Roberta!

(ROBERT-EARL *moves toward* ROBBIE. *But she raises her hand to signal him to stay away. They finally see* ROBBIE's *bloody hand.*)

(ROBERT-EARL *tries to approach* ROBBIE *but once again she gestures him away.*)

(*Then a searing pain races through her hand. Her face contorts. She cries out and drops her head, sobbing. She holds her bleeding hand. Blood continues to flow from the wound.*)

(ROBERT-EARL *scoops his daughter up in his arms. He gently kisses her forehead and rushes her to the bathroom.*)

(GERTIE *attempts to follow but he slams the door in her face.*)

(GERTIE *knocks at the door.*)

GERTIE: *(O S)* Robert Earl, Robert-Earl, please. Let me see about her.
(*She knocks. And knocks. No luck*)
(*She comes back in the living room.*)
(*She hesitates—then goes to the spot where her child bled.*)
(*She takes some napkins from the table and kneels down to wipe the blood away.*)
(*She reaches to clean the blood but stops—*)
(*She stares at* ROBBIE's *bloody handprint on the floor.*)
(*She is transfixed.*)

(*The phone rings again.*)

(*It startles* GERTIE. *She grabs her chest.*)
(*She quickly turns to look at the phone.*)

(*It rings again.*)

(*Abrupt black out*)

END OF PLAY